Violin   121VN

Jeremy Woolstenhulme

Welcome to learning vibrato! Adding vibrato to your playing is a perfect next step as you become a more advanced musician. You and the other members of your orchestra will learn together with step-by-step exercises and then you'll start adding vibrato to specially selected melodies and orchestral literature. Vibrato is a beautiful form of expression and helps to create new colors and timbres in music making like never before.

As you begin learning vibrato, review the following:

❏ Are you playing with proper overall posture?

❏ Is your left shoulder relaxed?

❏ Check your left hand, including your thumb. Relaxed?

❏ With your left hand in playing position, are your fingers, hand, and arm in proper alignment?

When starting the exercises on page 2, you will focus on left hand movement without and with the bow. As a violinist, you will have the option of working towards developing an arm vibrato or a wrist vibrato. Your teacher will guide you towards one type that's just right for you.

Use a metronome when practicing. ♩ = 70 is recommended for all exercises on pages 2-31. When you are getting started and practicing on your own, practice in short sessions. If you don't think something is feeling or looking right when practicing, consult with your teacher.

Vibrato Basics also includes short demonstration videos and they are available at no additional cost through the **Kjos INTERACTIVE Practice Studio** at *www.kjos.com.ips.* Details about accessing the **IPS** are provided on the inside front cover.

Best wishes and have fun!

Jeremy Woolstenhulme

ISBN-10: 0-8497-3556-4 • ISBN-13: 978-0-8497-3556-1

©2019 Kjos Music Press, Neil A. Kjos Music Company, Distributor, 4382 Jutland Drive, San Diego, California, 92117.
International copyright secured. All rights reserved. Printed in U.S.A.
WARNING! All music, photographs, graphics, and text are protected by copyright law.
To copy or reproduce them by any method is an infringement of the copyright law.
Anyone who reproduces copyrighted material is subject to substantial penalties and assessments for each infringement.

 and  are trademarks of Kjos Music Press.

2 Moving Arm or Wrist: NO BOW

Video Demo: Ex. 4

Arm Vibrato
Steps to Success:

- Place the violin in playing position.
- Slide your wrist back and forth a few inches along the side of the neck.
- Create the gliding movement along the neck by bending from the elbow.
- The vibrato motion is toward and away from your face. The arm does not rock from side to side!

Set your metronome to ♩ = 70 for all exercises on pages 2-31.

1.
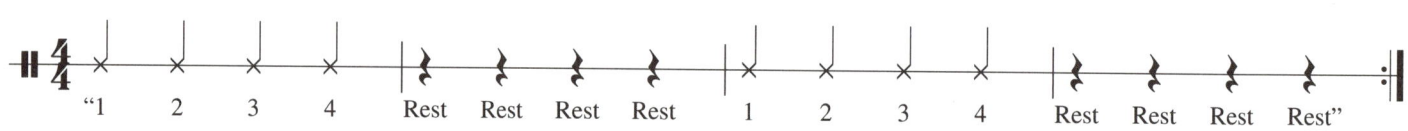

2.
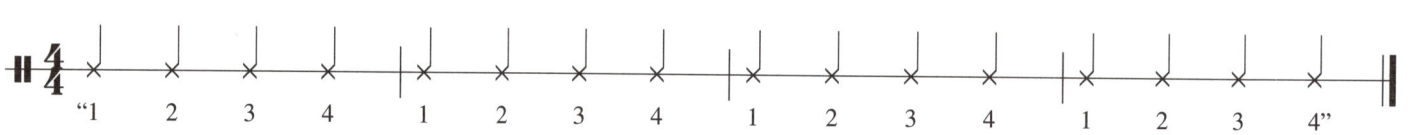

3.
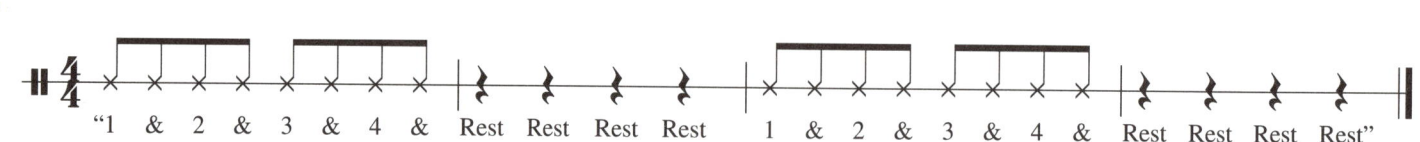

4. Video Demo
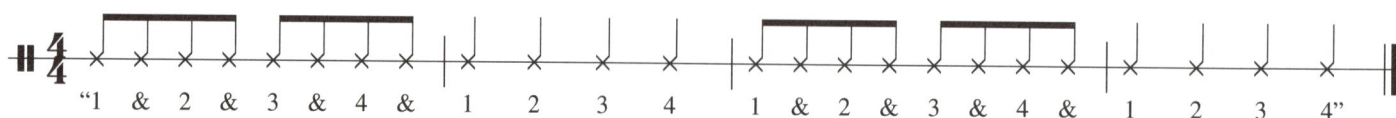

5.
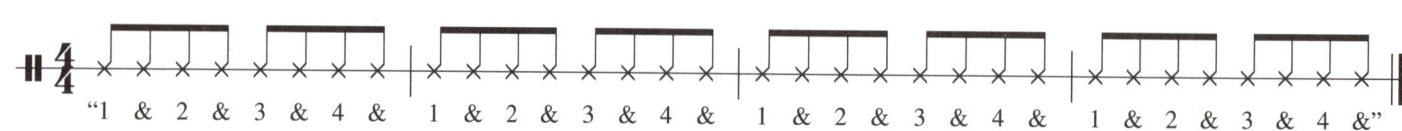

121VN

Moving Arm or Wrist: NO BOW

Wrist Vibrato
Steps to Success:

- ❑ Place the violin in playing position.
- ❑ Locate the thumb to the opposite side of the neck.
- ❑ Place wrist against the upper bout of the instrument to isolate the wrist.
- ❑ Bend only from the wrist so it looks like you are waving to yourself.
- ❑ The vibrato motion is toward and away from your face. Do not rock the wrist from side to side!

6.
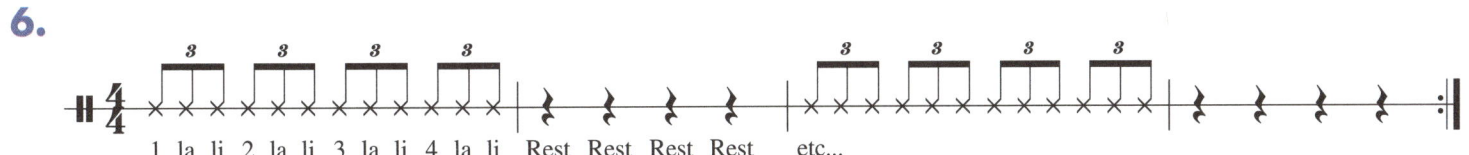

7.
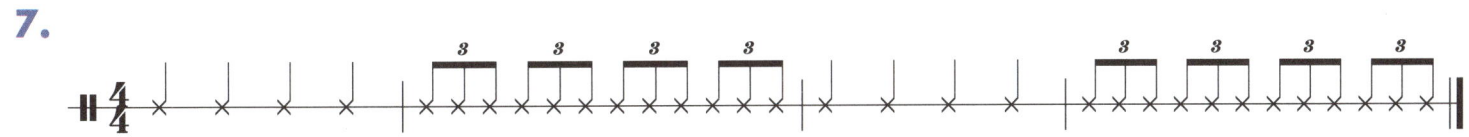

8.
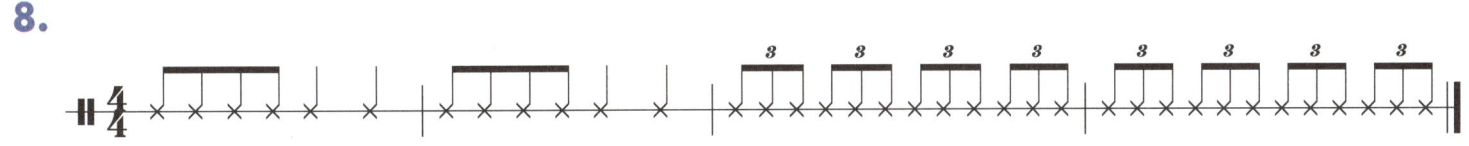

9.
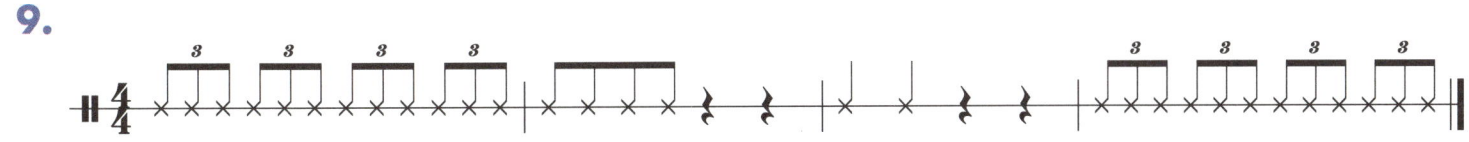

10.
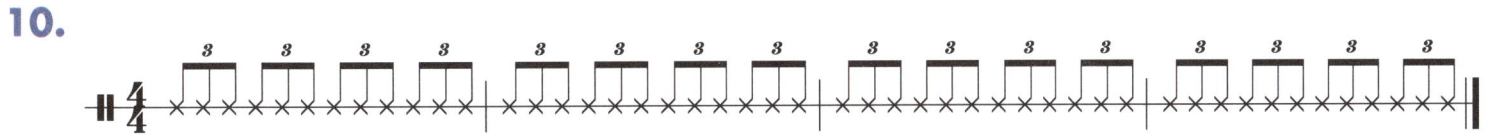

4 Moving Arm or Wrist: WITH BOW

Video Demo: Ex. 14

Steps to Success:
- Add the bow by playing arco on the open D string.
- At the same time, have your left arm or wrist execute the same movements learned on pages 2 and 3.
- Count aloud.

11.

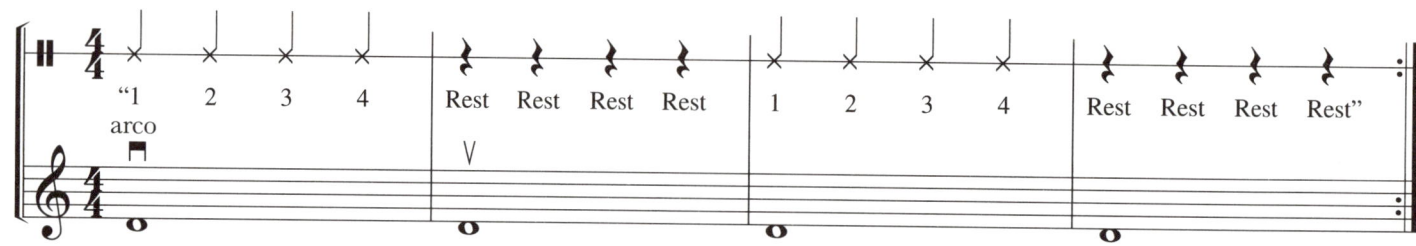

12.

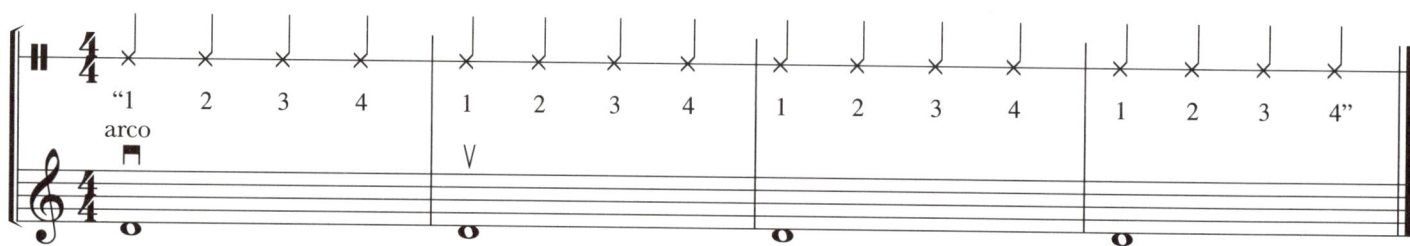

13.

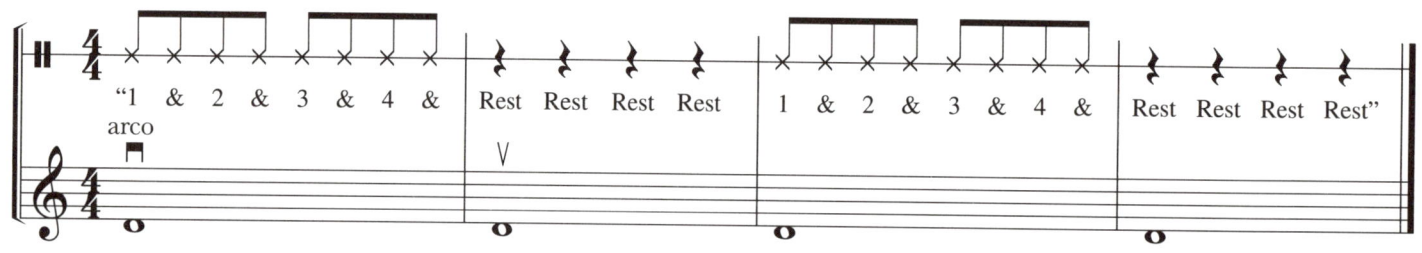

VIDEO DEMO

14.

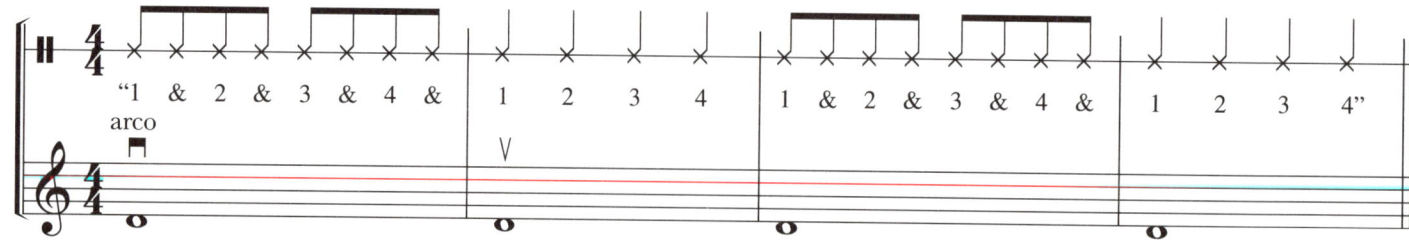

15.

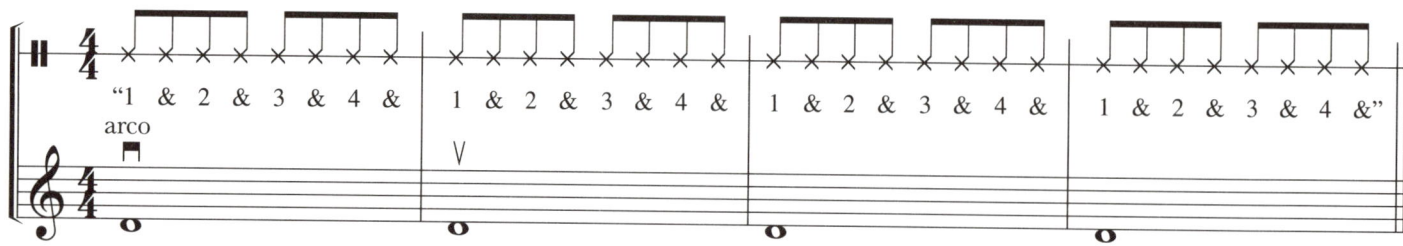

121VN

Moving Arm or Wrist: WITH BOW

16.
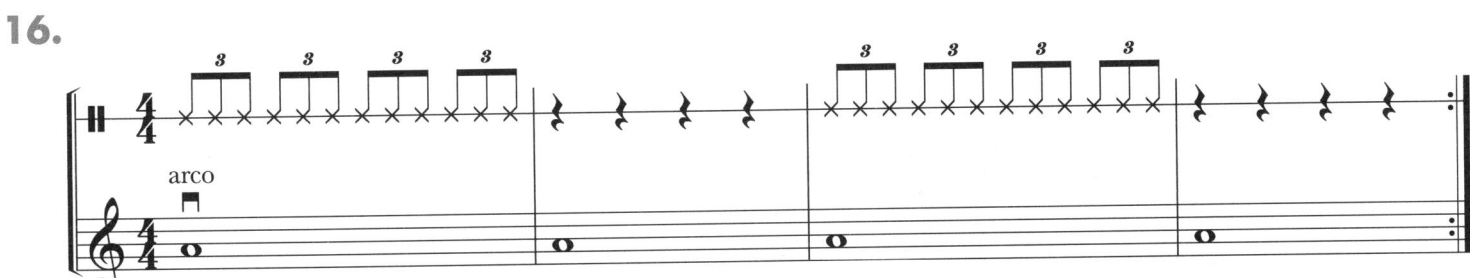

17.
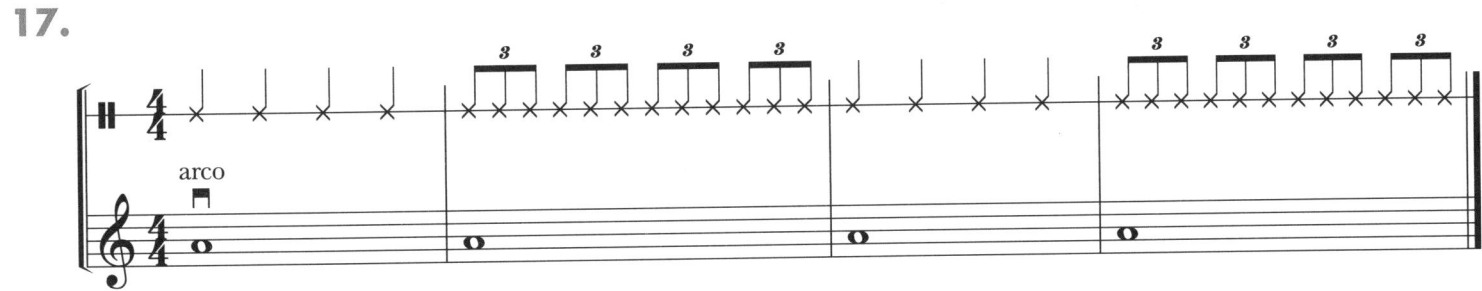

18.
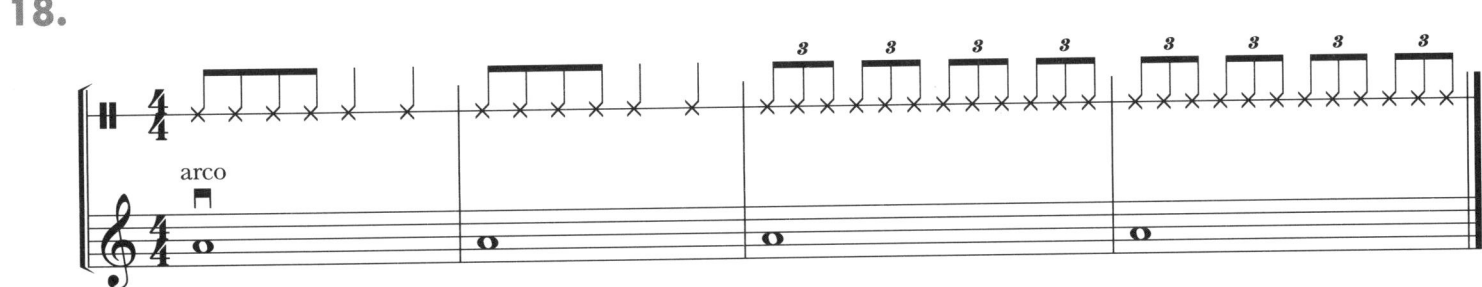

19.
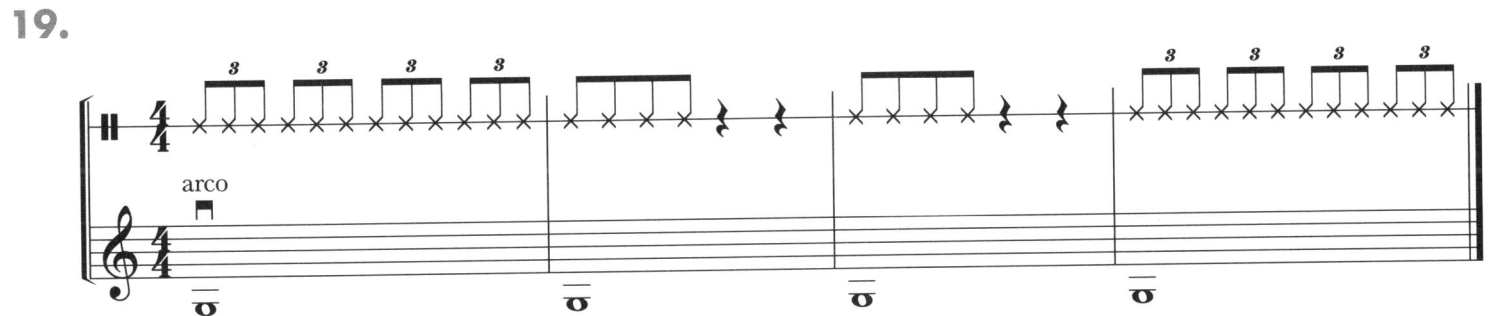

20.
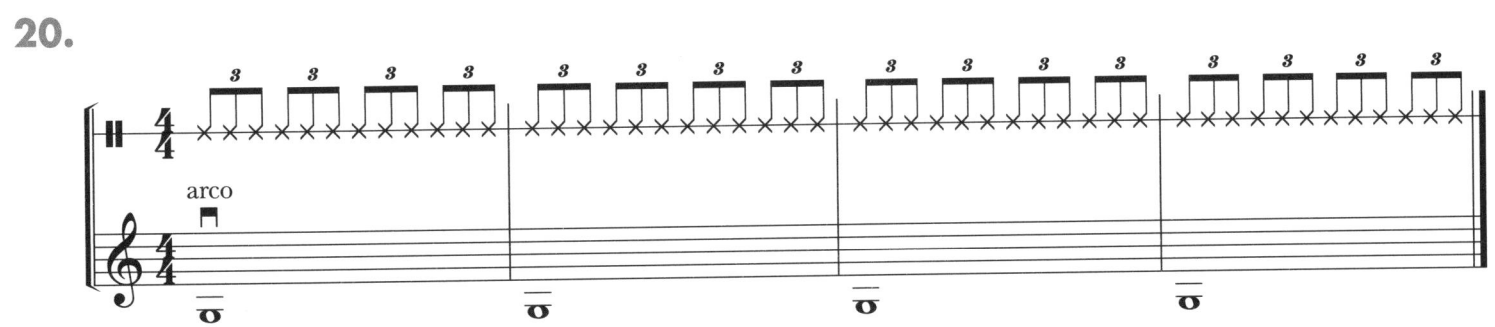

121VN

6 Stationary Thumb Movement: NO BOW

🎥 Video Demo: Ex. 24

Arm Vibrato
Steps to Success:

❏ Place the pad of the thumb against the neck of the violin.
❏ Move the knuckle away from the neck so that it does not inhibit the vibrato movement. The thumb pad is the only thing to touch the neck.
❏ While hovering the fingers over the strings, move from the elbow so that the hand rocks back and forth over the strings. The thumb pad is stationary.
❏ The vibrato motion is toward and away from your face. Do not rock the wrist from side to side!

Reminder: The pulse of all exercises should be ♩ = 70.

21.

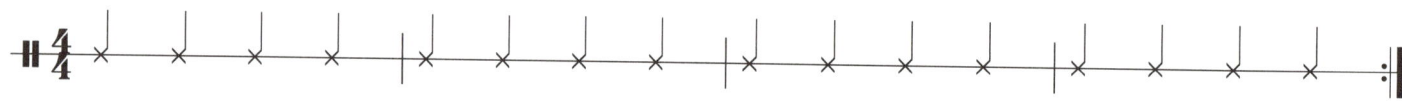

22.

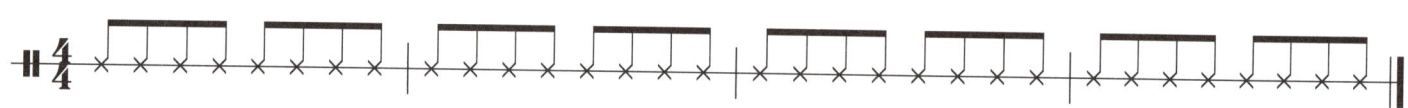

23.

24. Video Demo

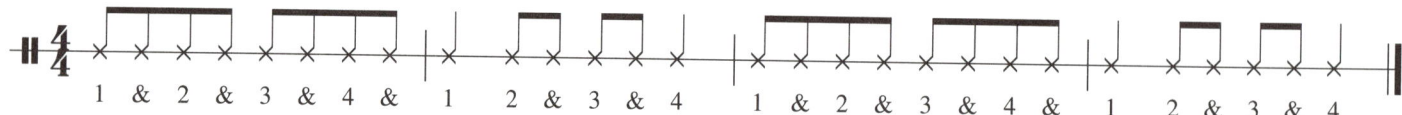

1 & 2 & 3 & 4 &   1   & 2 & 3 & 4   1 & 2 & 3 & 4 &   1   2 & 3 & 4

25.

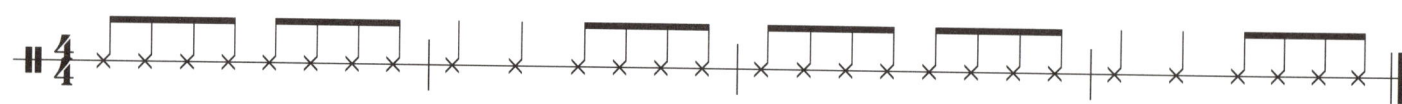

Stationary Thumb Movement: NO BOW

Wrist Vibrato
Steps to Success:

❏ Place the pad of the thumb against the neck of the violin.

❏ Move the knuckle away from the neck so that it does not inhibit the vibrato movement. The thumb pad is the only thing to touch the neck.

❏ While hovering the fingers over the strings, move from the wrist so that the hand rocks back and forth over the strings. The thumb pad is stationary.

❏ The vibrato motion is toward and away from your face. Do not rock the wrist from side to side!

26.

27.
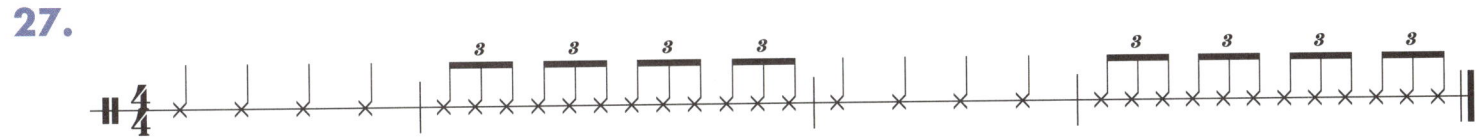

28.
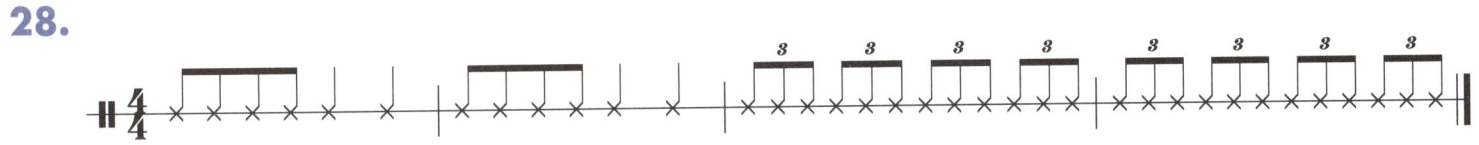

29.
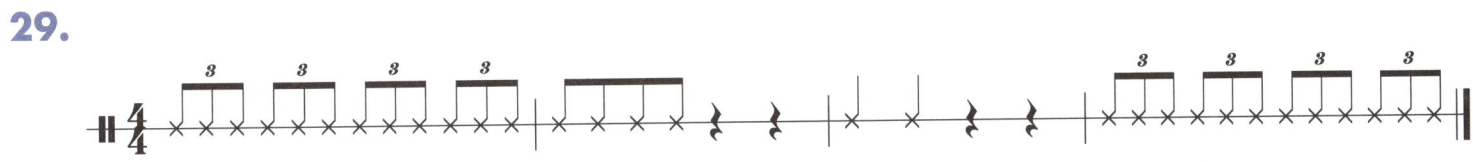

30.
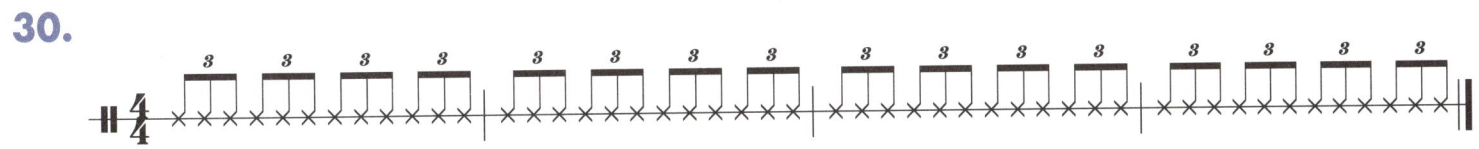

121VN

8 Stationary Thumb Movement: WITH BOW

Video Demo: Ex. 34

Arco open string, left arm doing vibrato movements from top line.
Count aloud when bowing open strings.

31.

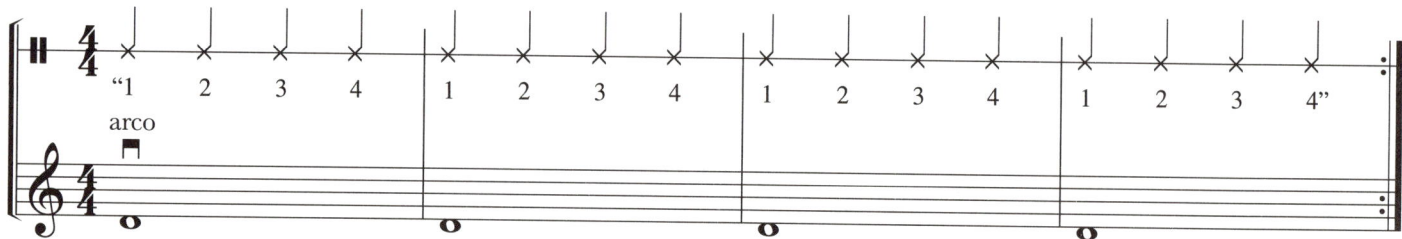

32.

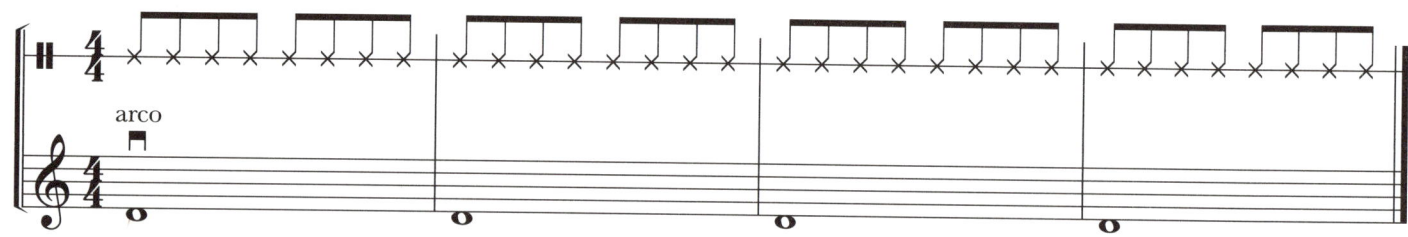

33.

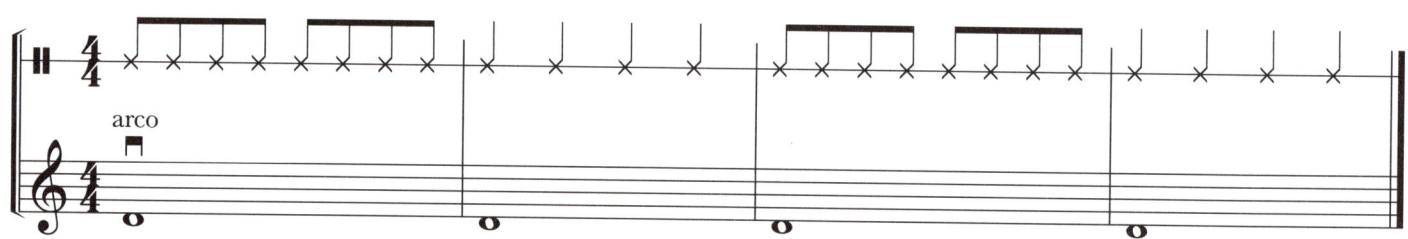

34. Video Demo

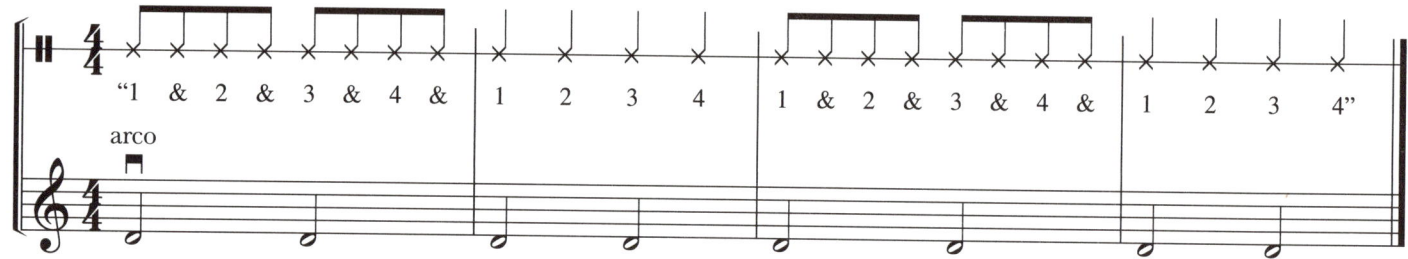

35.

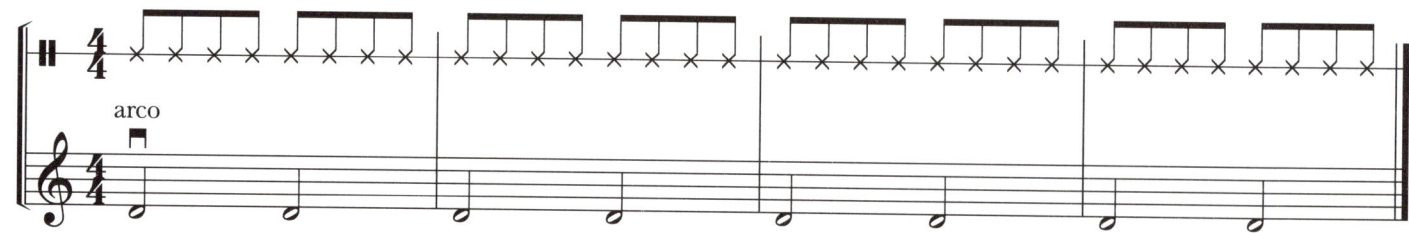

121VN

Stationary Thumb Movement: WITH BOW

36.

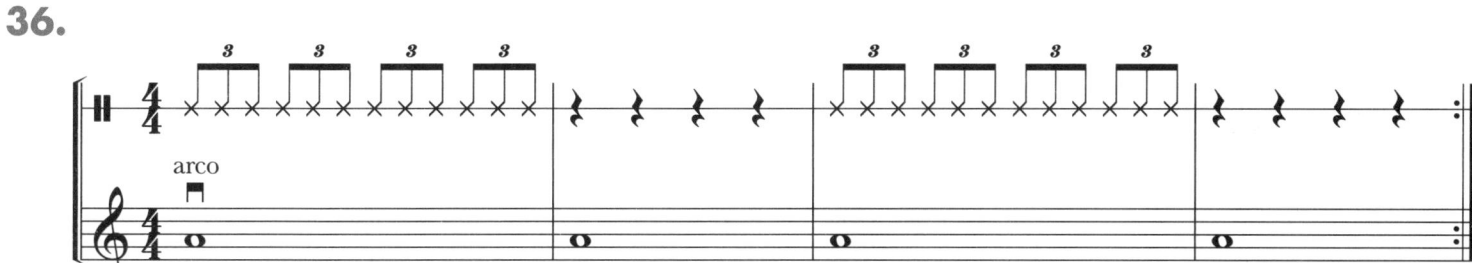

37.

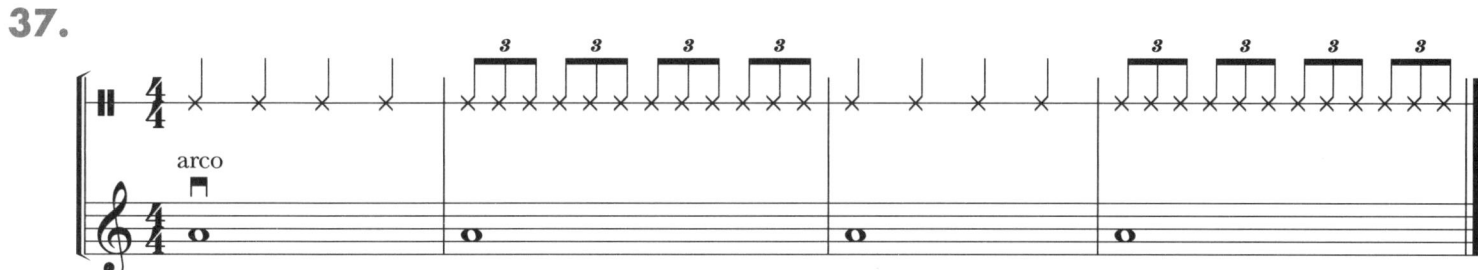

38.

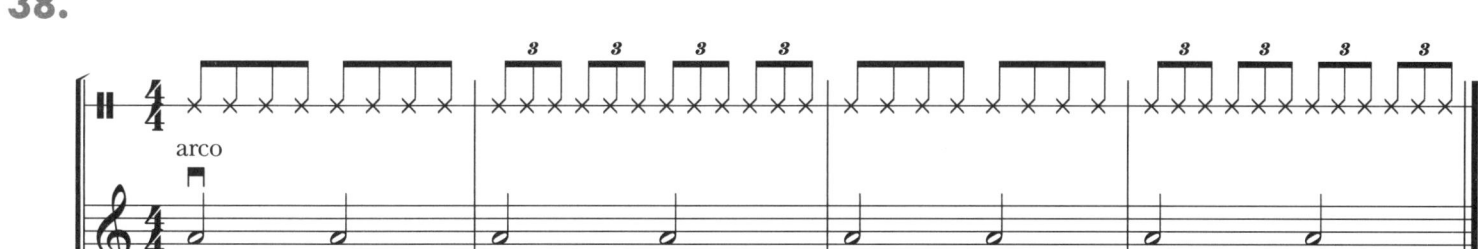

39.

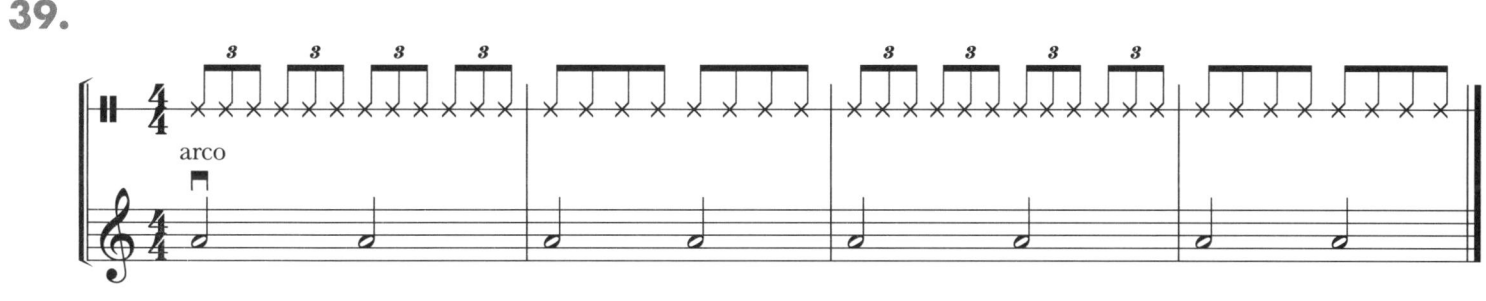

40.

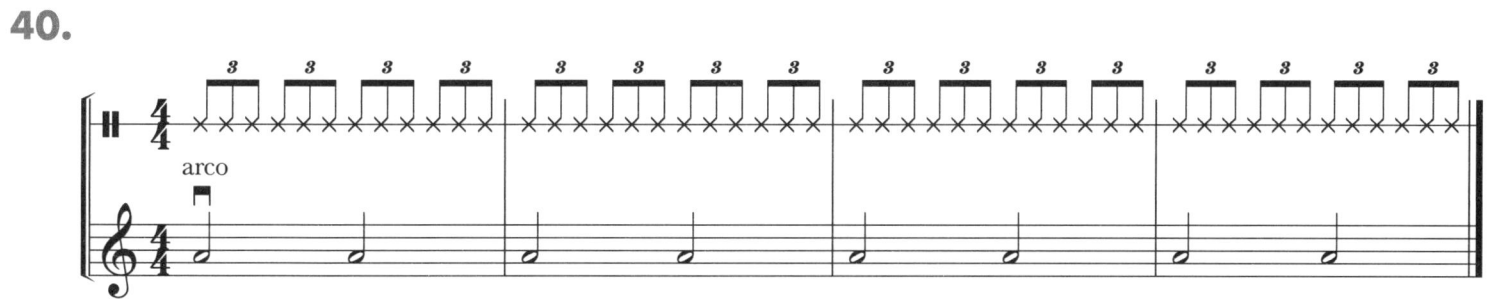

10 Finger Bend on the Purfling of the Upper Bout: NO BOW

Video Demo: Ex. 44

Arm Vibrato
Steps to Success:

❏ Move the palm against the upper bout of the violin.

❏ Place the tip of the finger on the purfling, the black stripes around the top of the instrument.

❏ Place thumb as an anchor to the hand around the end of the neck.

❏ Move the elbow to rock the finger back and forth while the tip of the finger stays fixed on the purfling.

Start with the 2nd finger or 3rd finger. Try others too. The focus is on movement.

41.
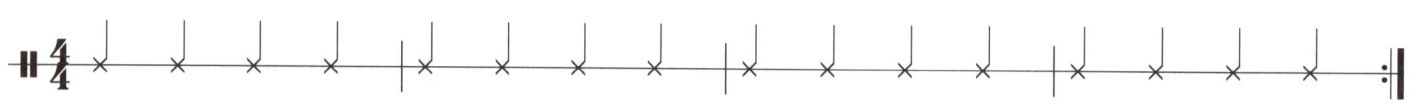

42.
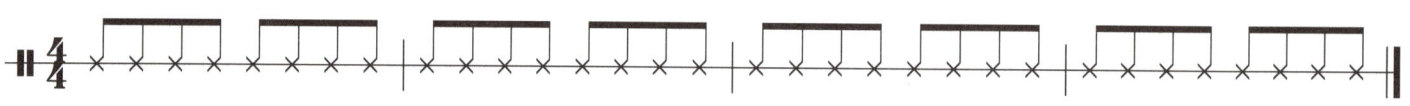

43.
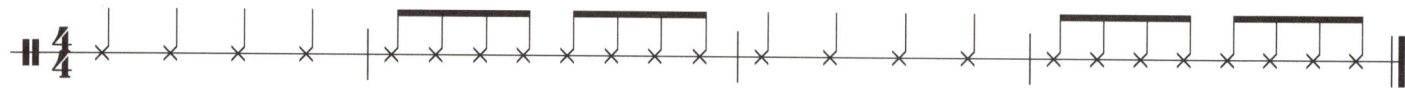

VIDEO DEMO

44.
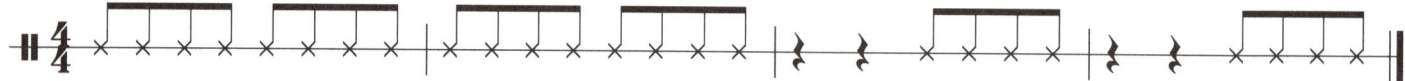

45.

121VN

Finger Bend on the Purfling of the Upper Bout: NO BOW

**Wrist Vibrato
Steps to Success:**

❑ Move the palm against the upper bout of the violin.

❑ Place the tip of the finger on the purfling, the black stripes around the top of the instrument.

❑ Place thumb as an anchor to the hand around the end of the neck.

❑ Move the wrist to rock the finger back and forth while the tip of the finger stays fixed on the purfling.

Start with the 2nd finger or 3rd finger. Try others too. The focus is on movement.

46.

47.

48.

49.

50.

12 Finger Bend on the Purfling of the Upper Bout: WITH BOW
Video Demo: Ex. 54

51.
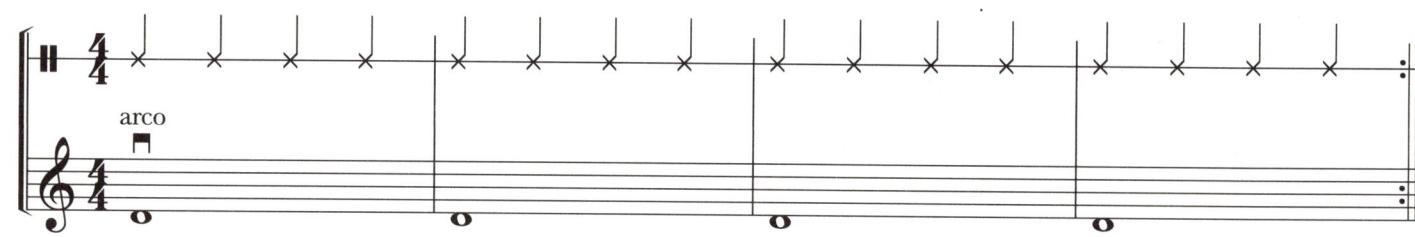

52.
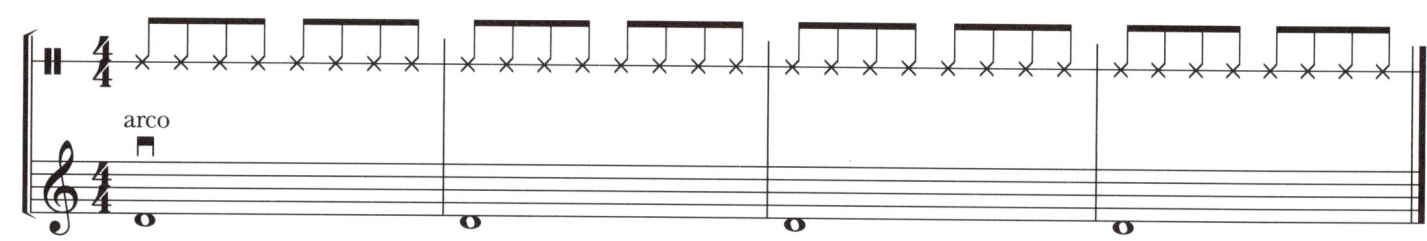

53.
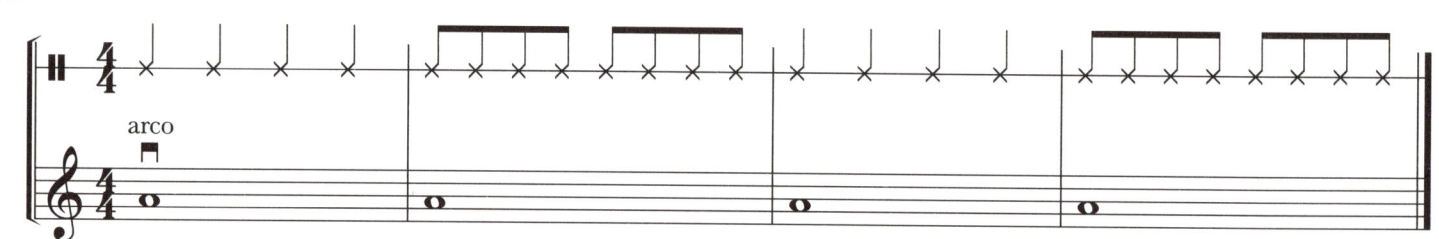

54. VIDEO DEMO
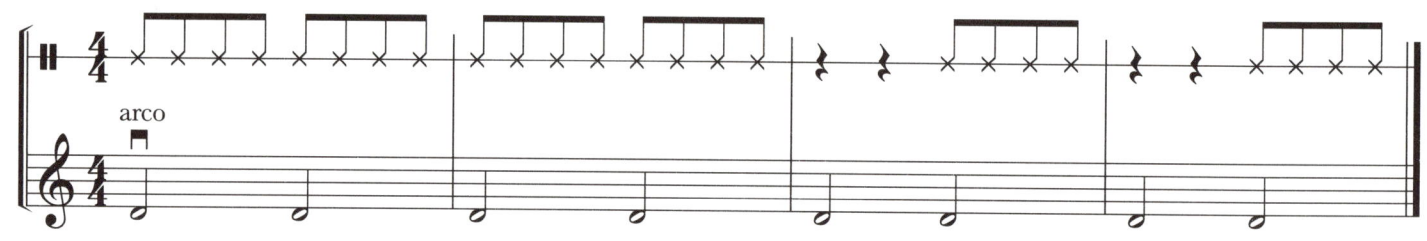

55.
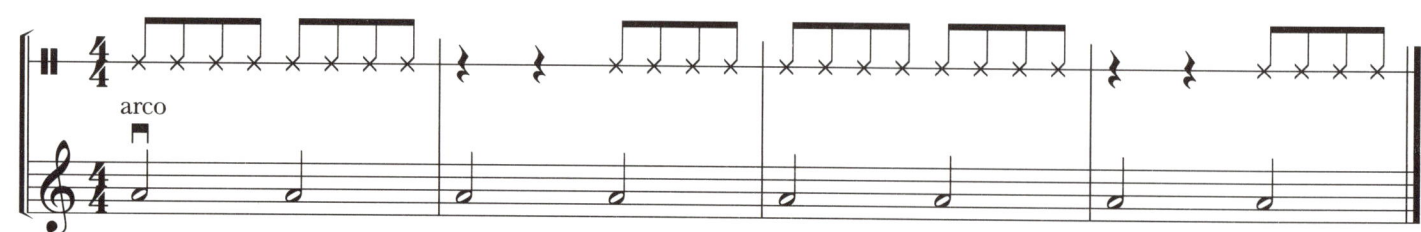

121VN

Finger Bend on the Purfling of the Upper Bout: WITH BOW

56.
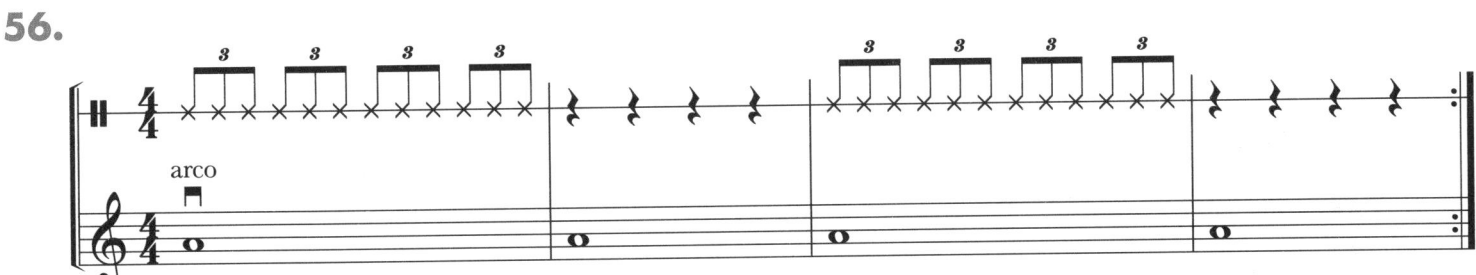

57.
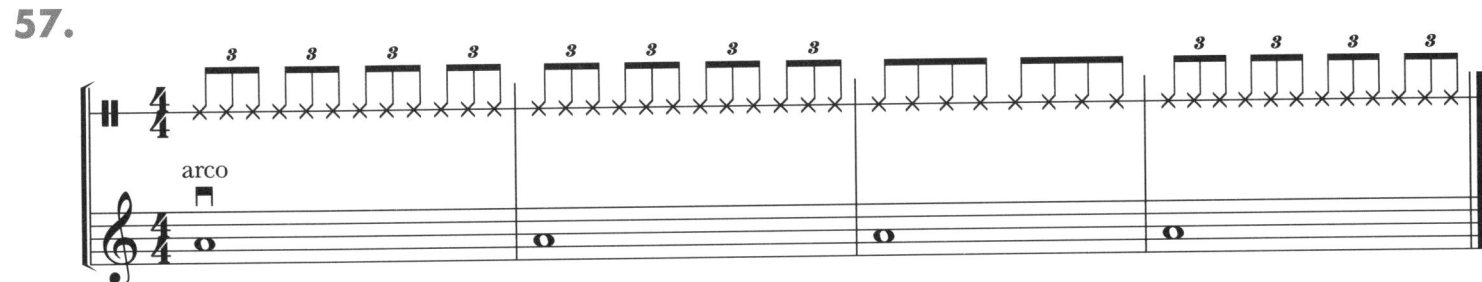

58.
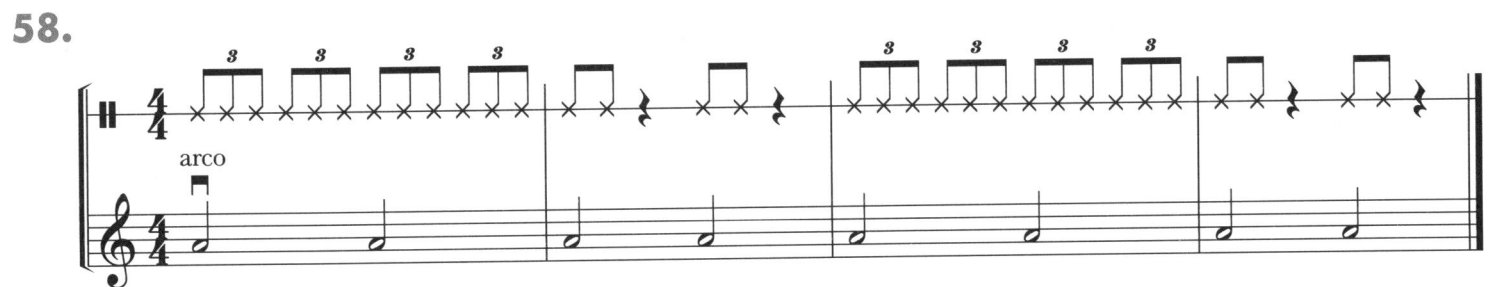

59.

60.
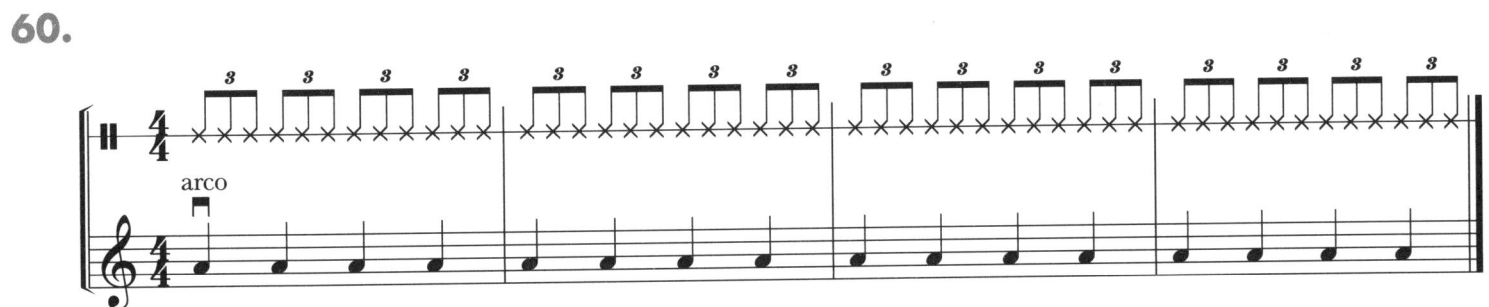

14 String Polish Movement: NO BOW

Video Demo: Ex. 64

Arm Vibrato
Steps to Success:

- Lightly place the finger on the string.
- Move the elbow so the finger lightly slides back and forth along the string.
- The polish movements should only be about an inch in length. There is no need to move too far along the neck.
- The thumb should rock back and forth but keep the pad of the thumb fixed to the neck.
- The knuckle should be pulled away from the neck to insure free movement of the hand.

Start with the 2nd finger or 3rd finger. Try others too. The focus is on movement.

61.
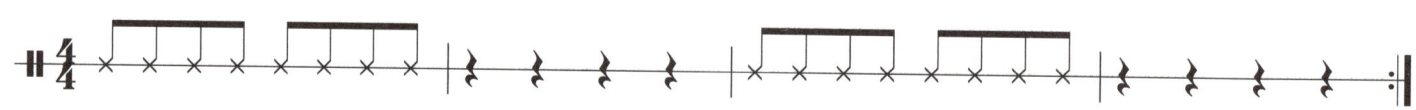

62.
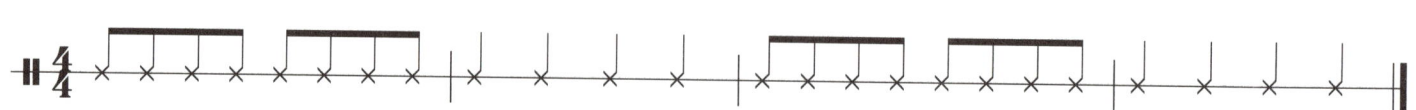

63.
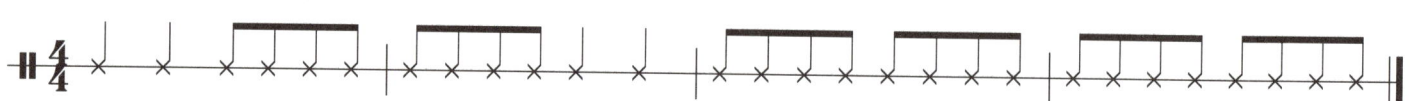

64. VIDEO DEMO
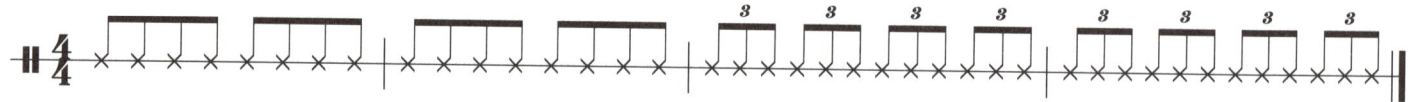

65.
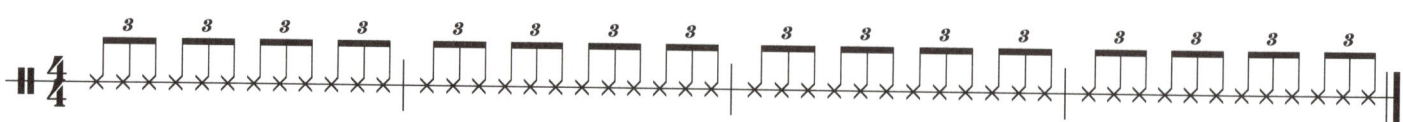

String Polish Movement: NO BOW

**Wrist Vibrato
Steps to Success:**

❑ Lightly place the finger on the string.

❑ Move the wrist so the finger lightly slides back and forth along the string.

❑ The polish movements should only be about an inch in length. There is no need to move too far along the neck.

❑ The thumb should rock back and forth but keep the pad of the thumb fixed to the neck.

❑ The knuckle should be pulled away from the neck to insure free movement of the hand.

66.

"1 e & a 2 e & a 3 e & a 4 e & a Rest Rest Rest Rest   1 e & a 2 e & a 3 e & a 4 e & a Rest Rest Rest Rest"

67.

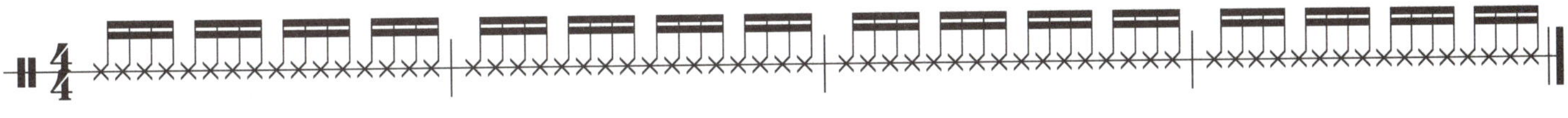

68.

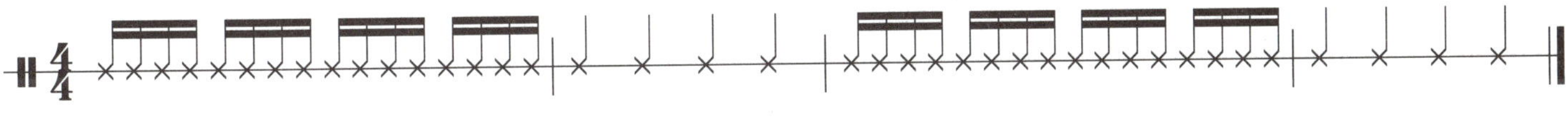

69.

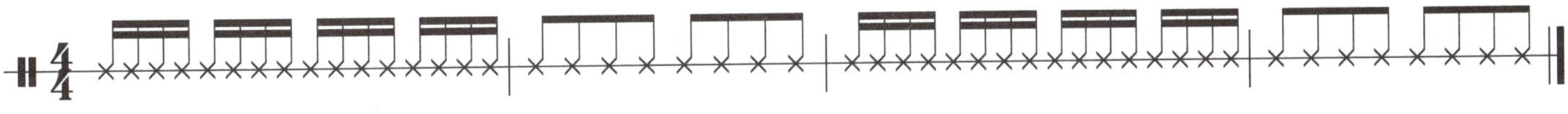

70.

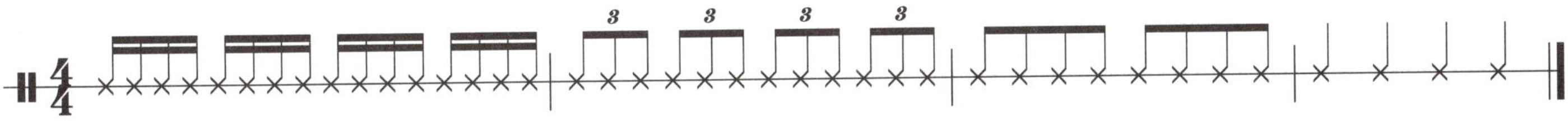

16 String Polish Movement: WITH BOW

Video Demo: Ex. 75

71.
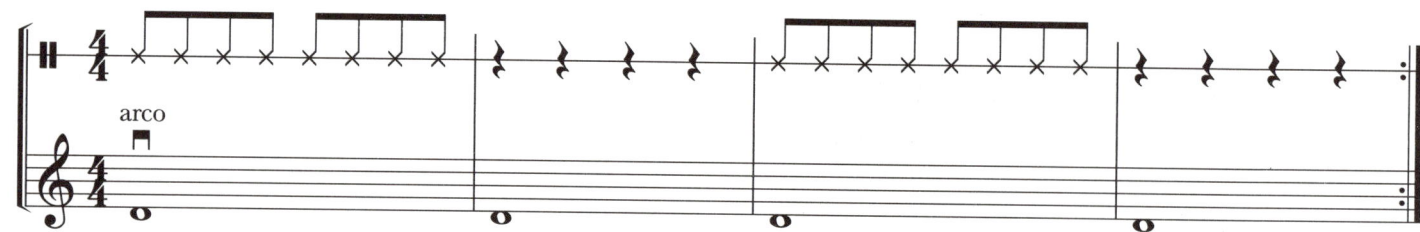

72.
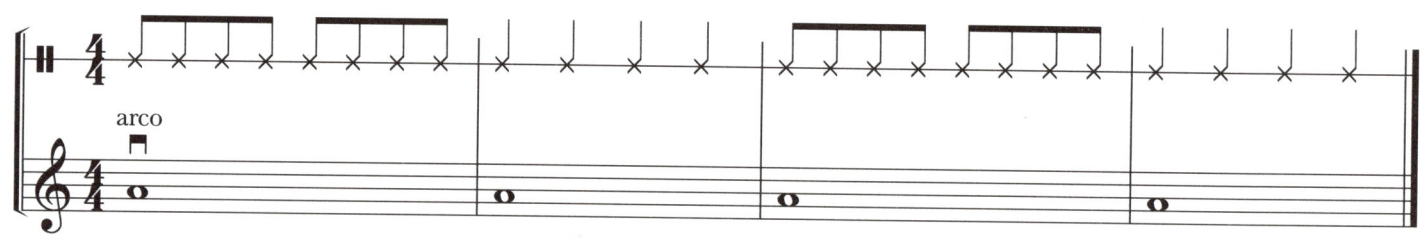

73.
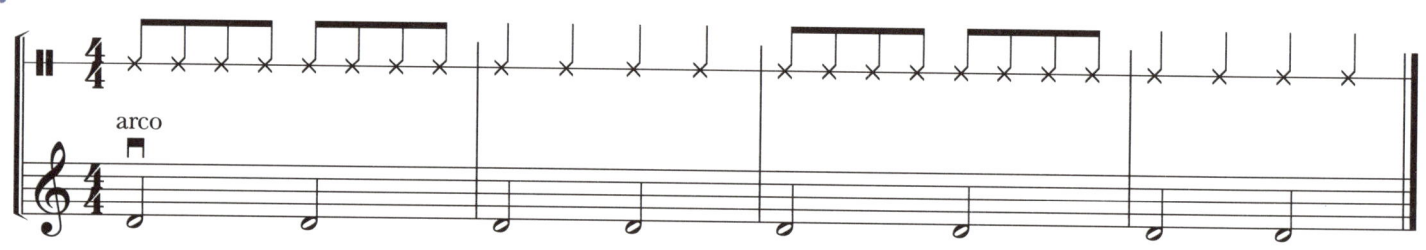

74.
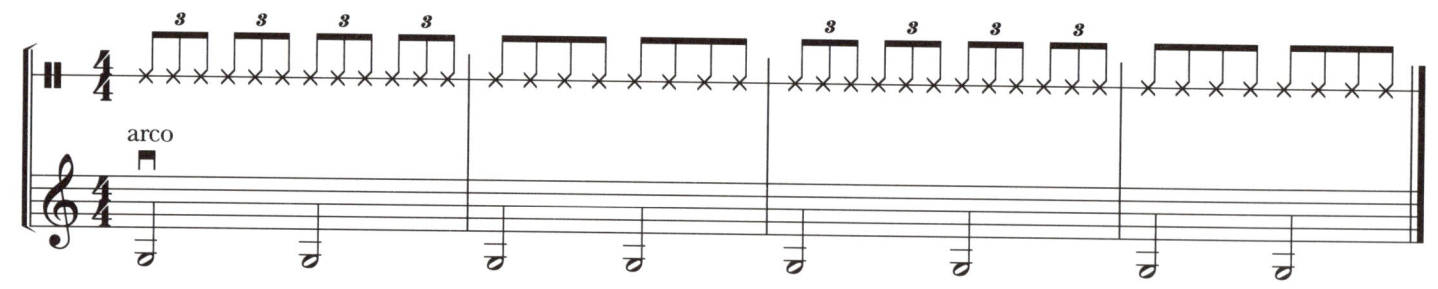

VIDEO DEMO

75.
Polish on different strings!
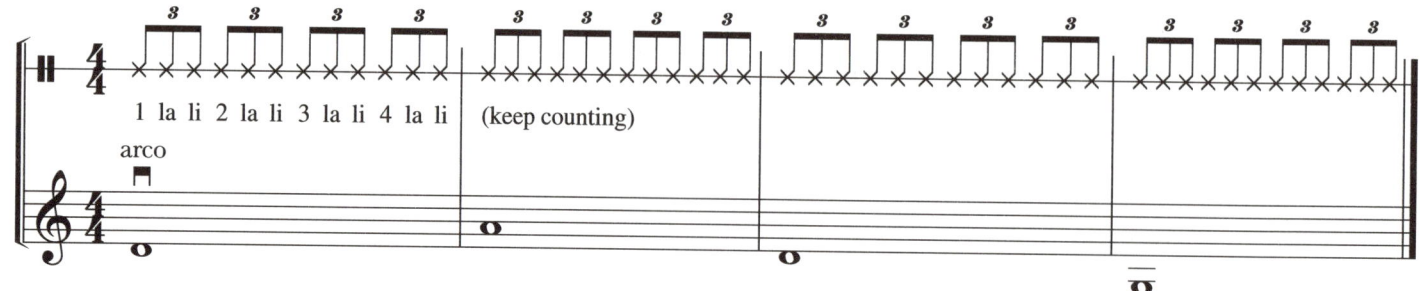

1 la li 2 la li 3 la li 4 la li   (keep counting)

String Polish Movement: WITH BOW

17

Exercises 76, 77, and 80 include polish on different strings.

76.
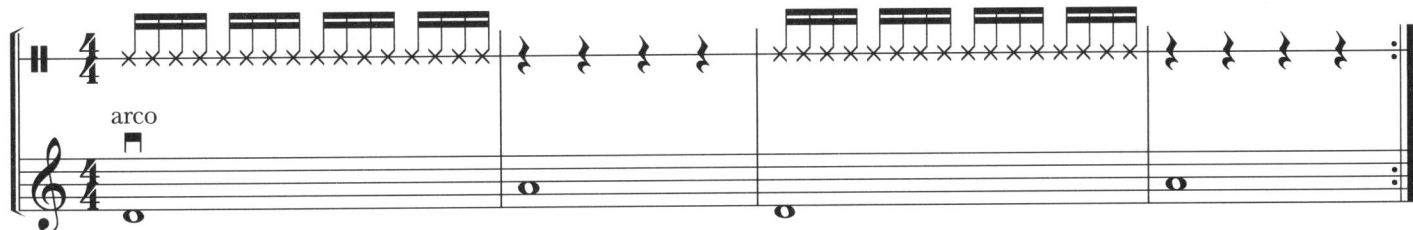

77.
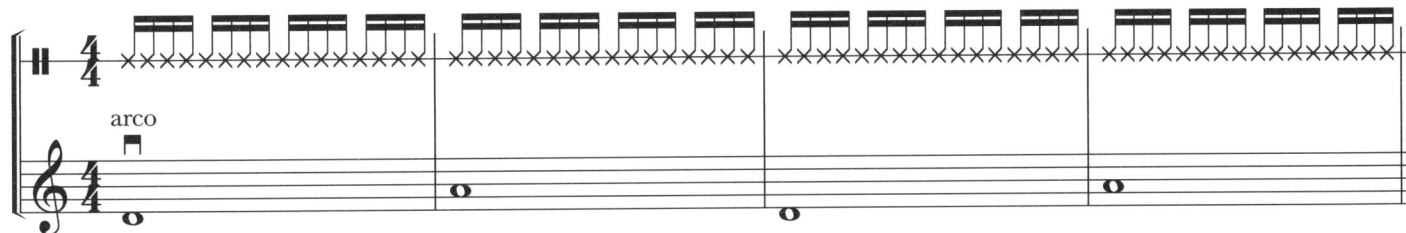

78.
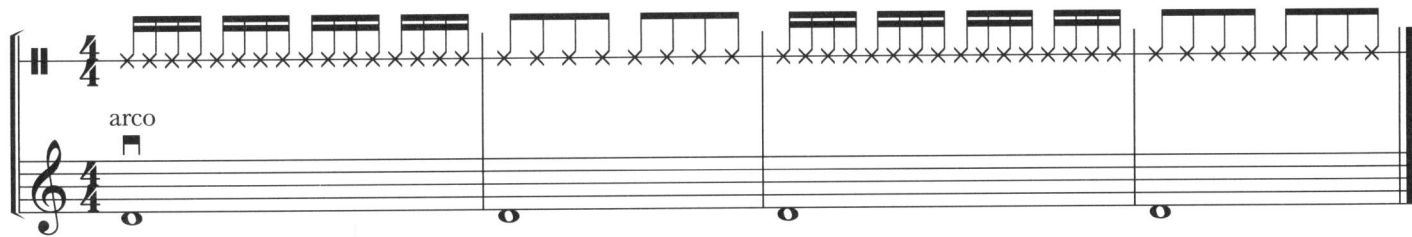

79.
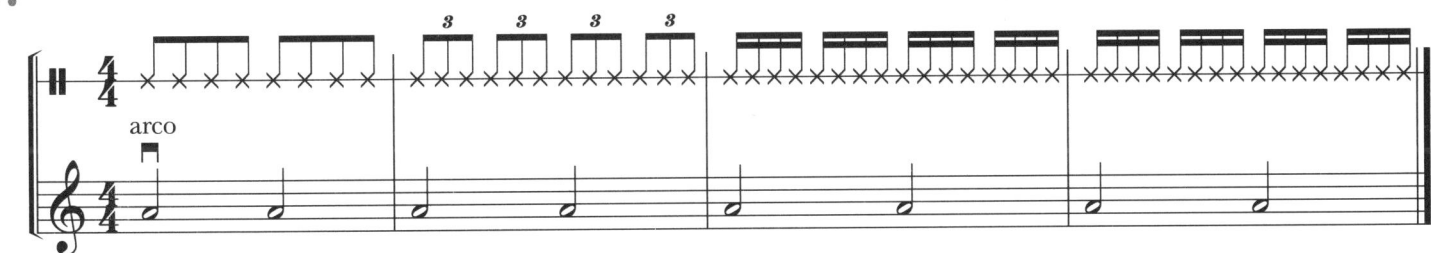

80.
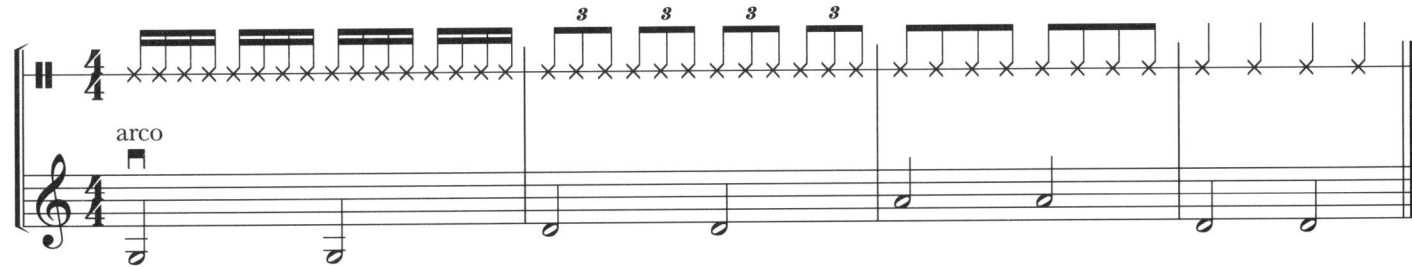

121VN

18 Finger Rock: NO BOW & WITH BOW

 **Video Demo: Ex. 82**

First try without the bow, then add the bow using whole notes.

81.

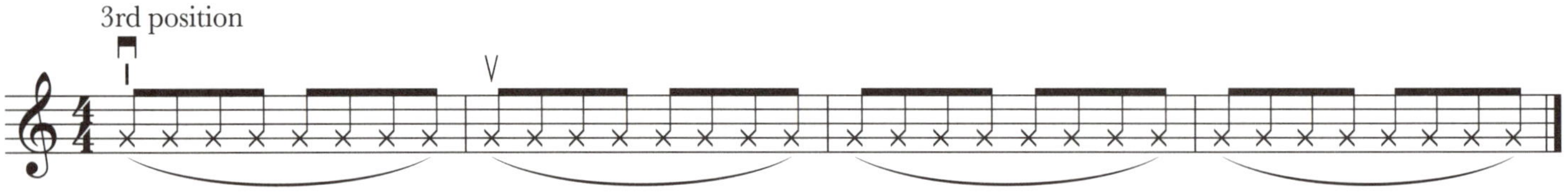

82. VIDEO DEMO

1 & 2 & 3 & 4 & (keep counting)

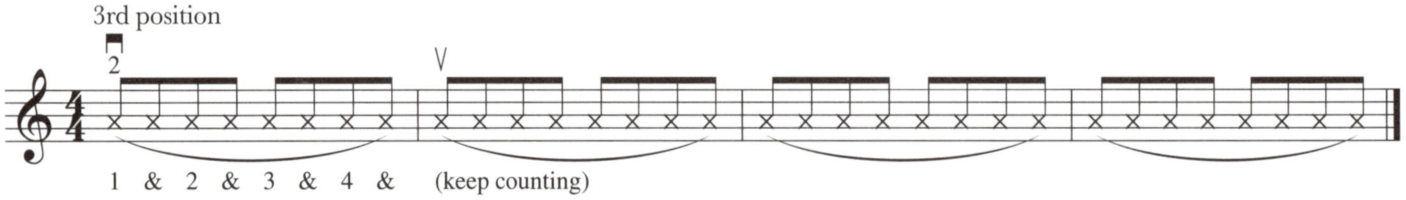

83.

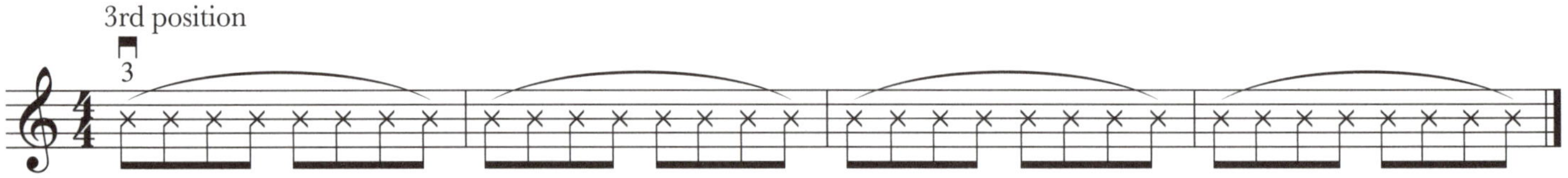

84.

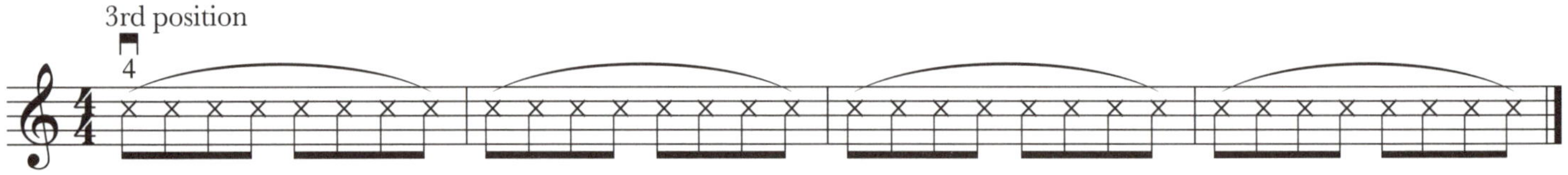

85.

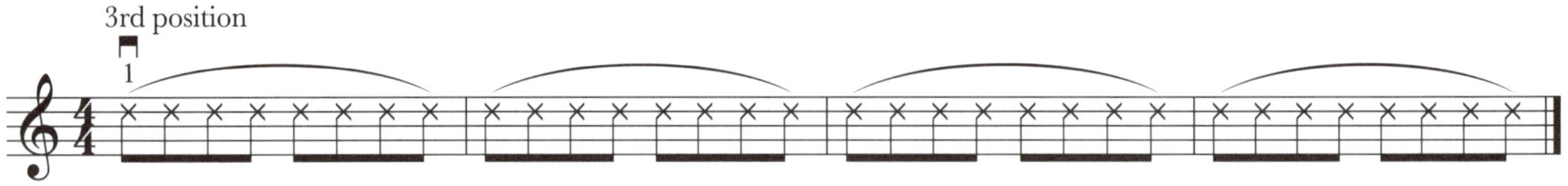

86.

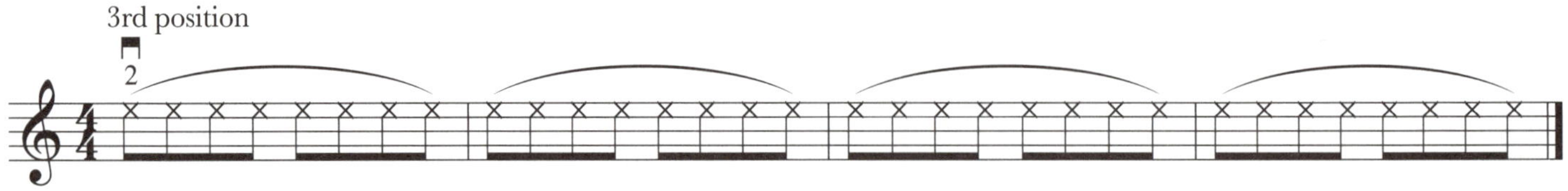

87.

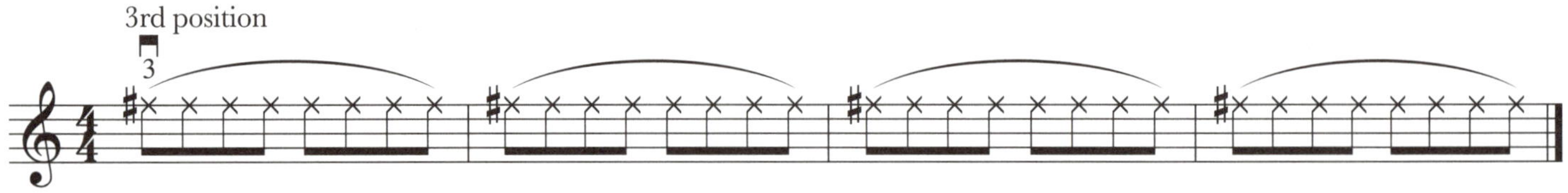

88.

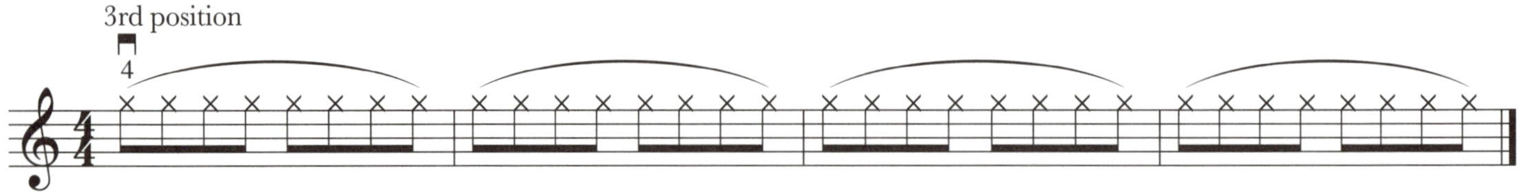

Finger Rock: NO BOW & WITH BOW

19

Play exercises 89-96 in 1st position.

89.
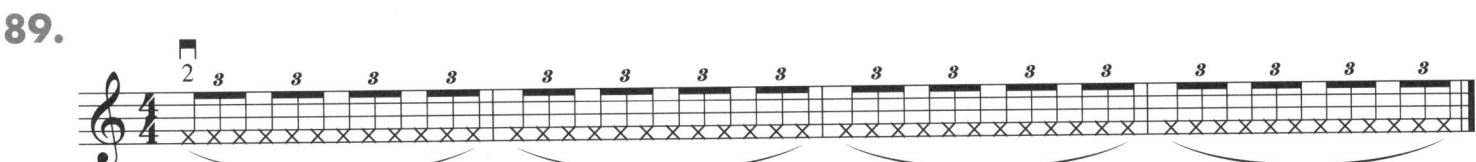

90.
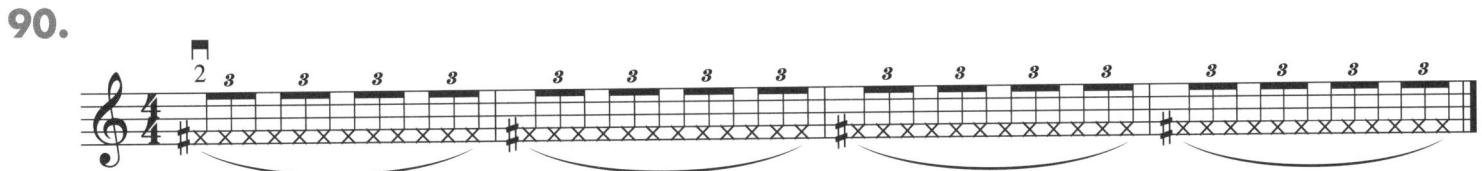

91.
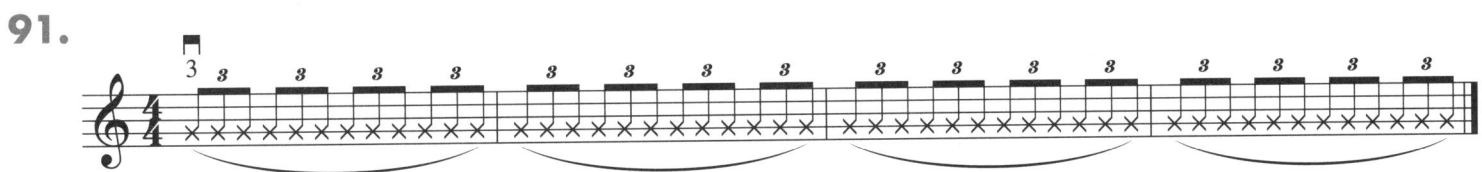

92.
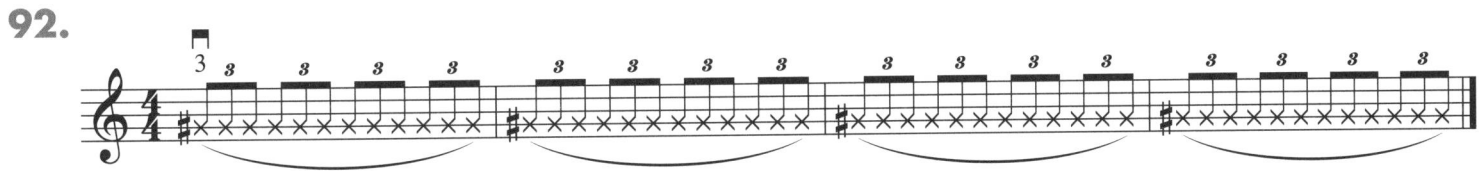

93.
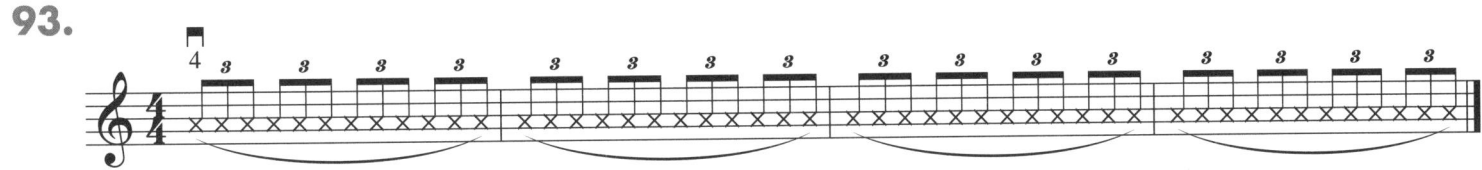

94.
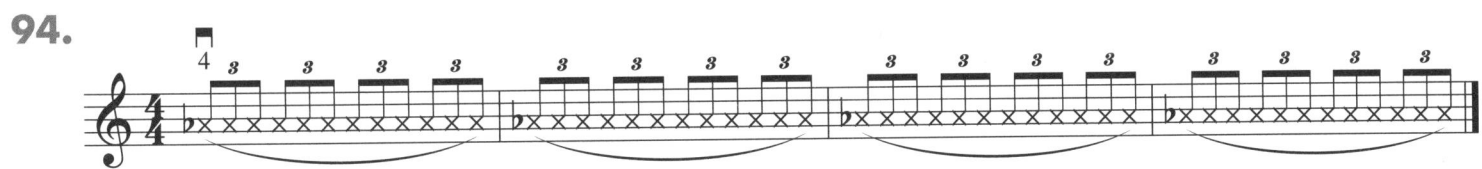

95.
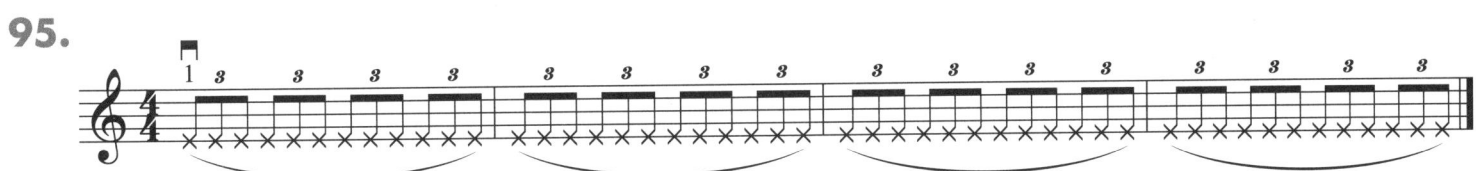

96.
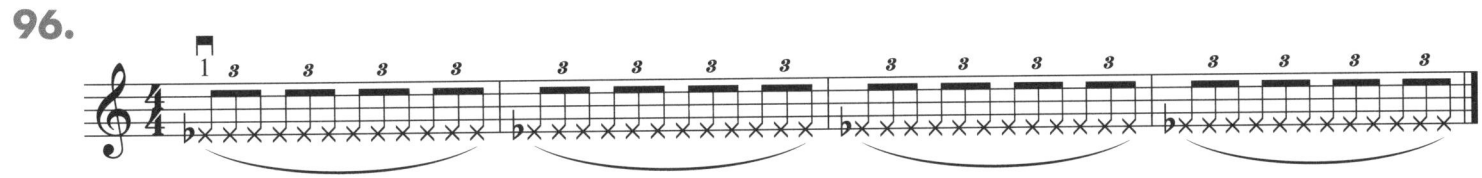

121VN

20 Polish to Plant: WITH BOW

Video Demo: Ex. 97

Polish to Plant: WITH BOW

22 Steady Vibrato Speed

Video Demo: Ex. 113-115

113.

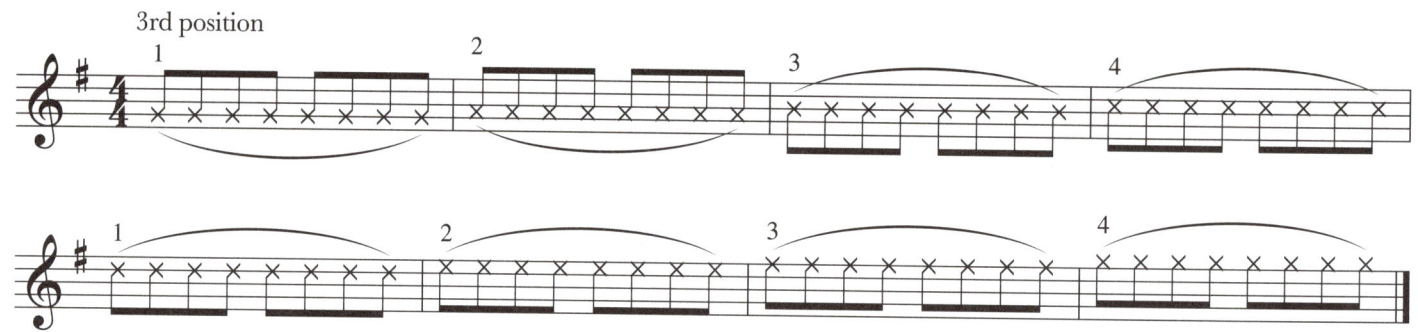

114.

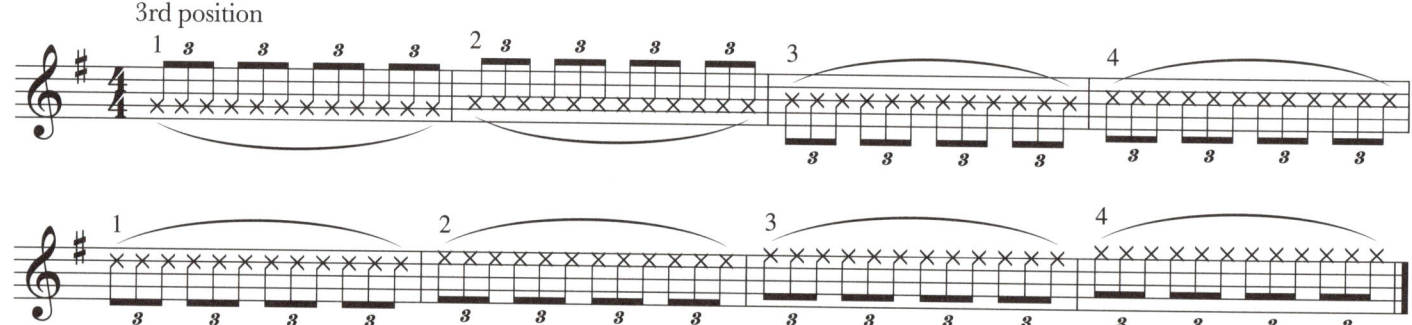

115.

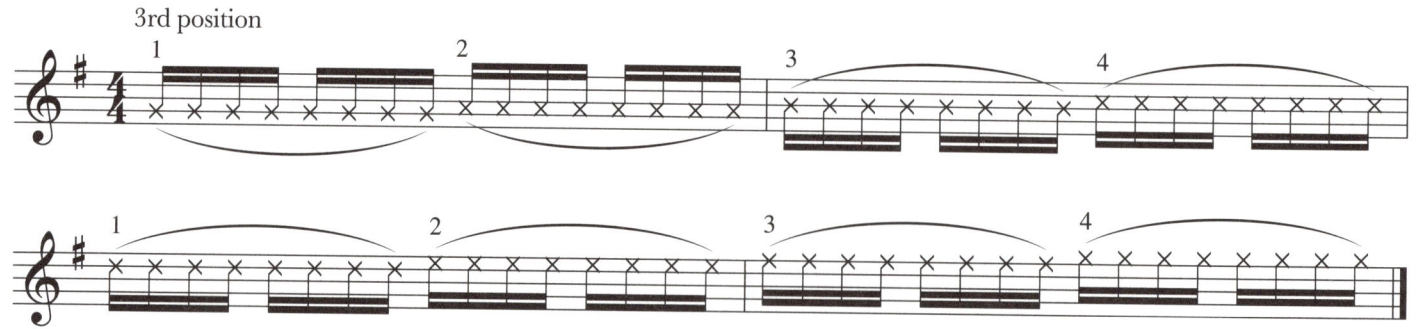

116. Achieve a rhythmic and steady vibrato.
[G major scale in 3rd position]

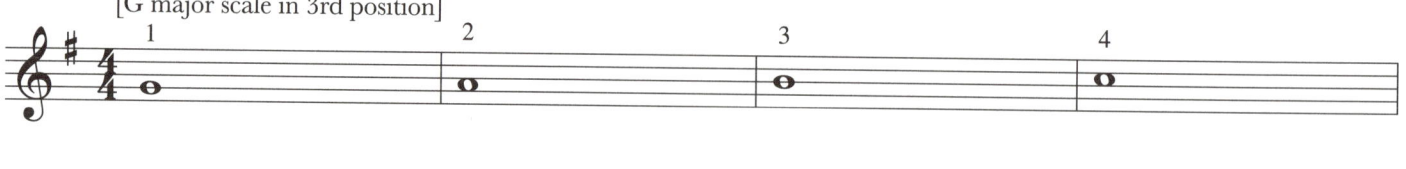

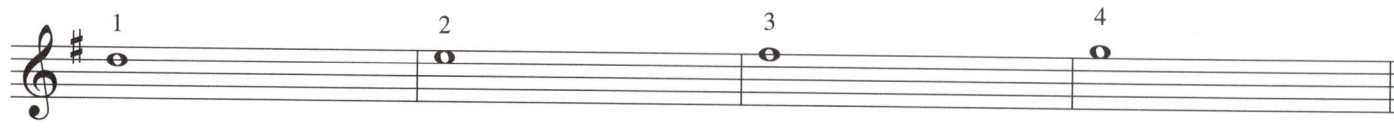

Steady Vibrato Speed

117.

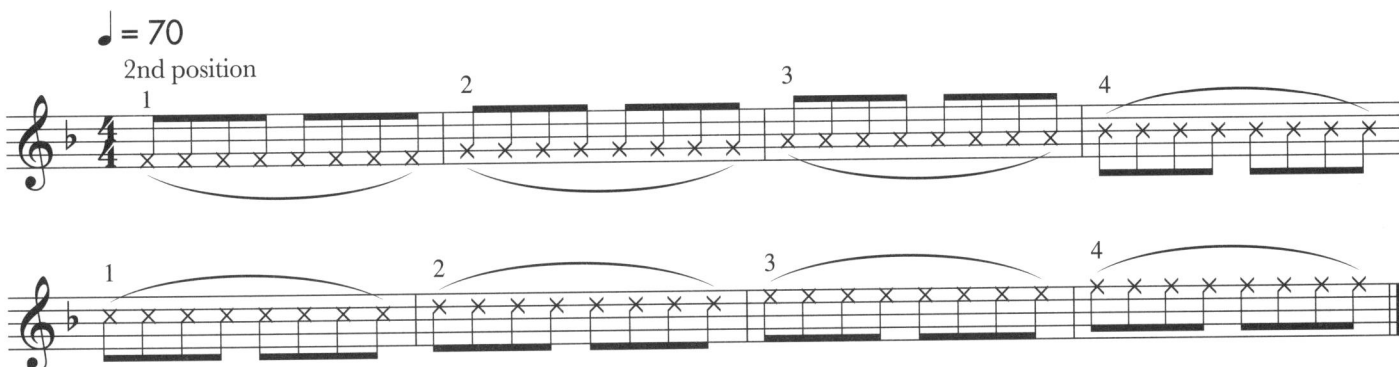

118.

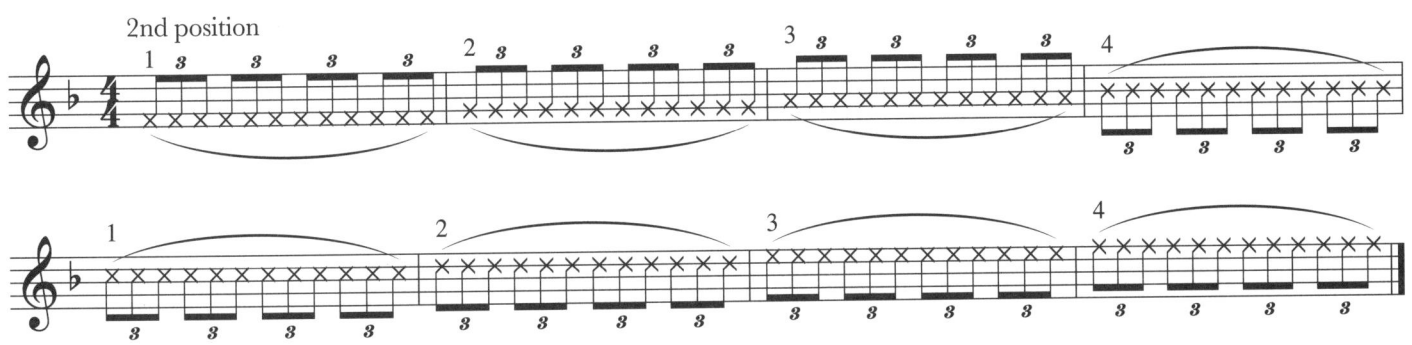

119.

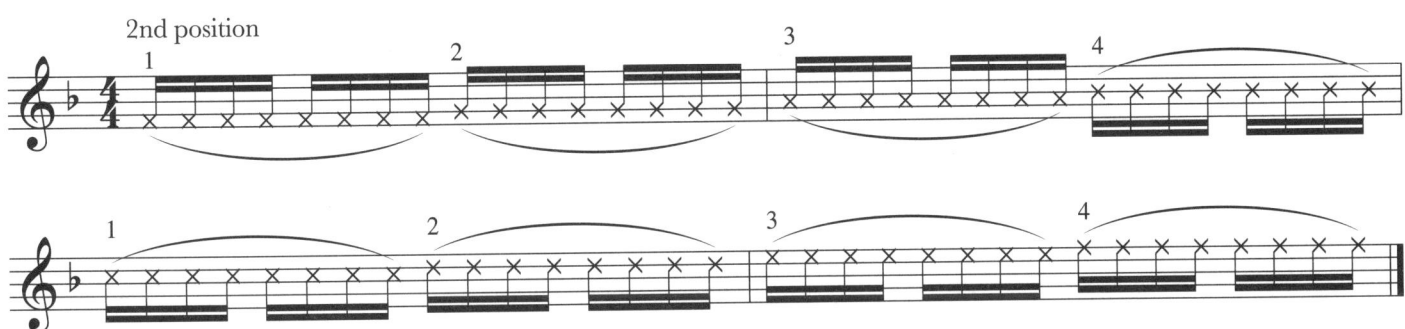

120.

Achieve a rhythmic and steady vibrato.
[F major scale in 2nd position]

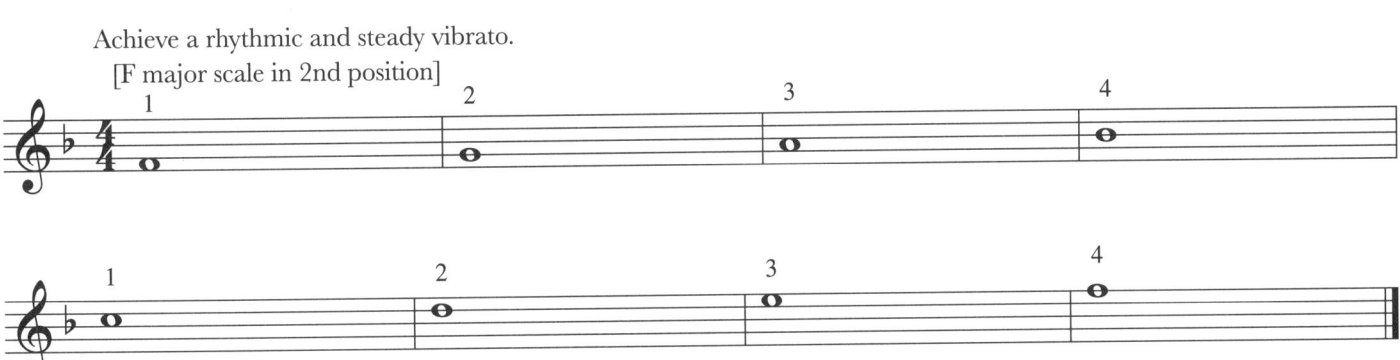

24 Constant Vibrato Speed

Play each line with a slow and steady vibrato.

121.
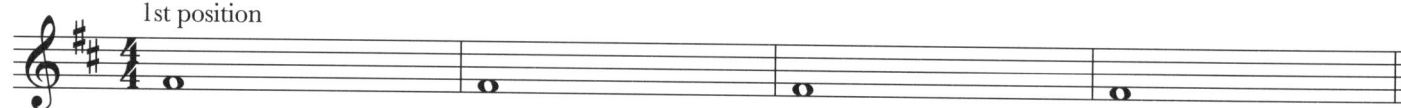

122.
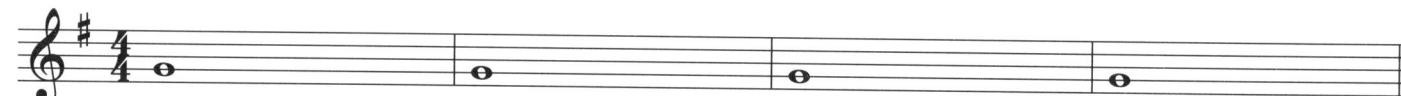

123.
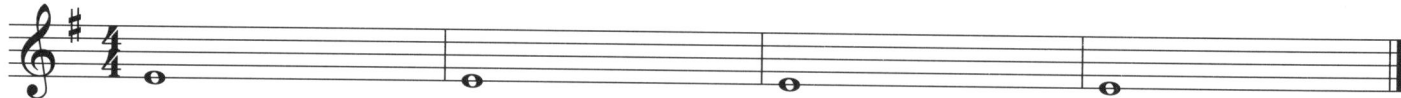

124.

125.
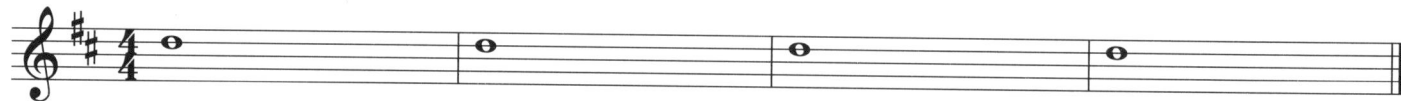

126.
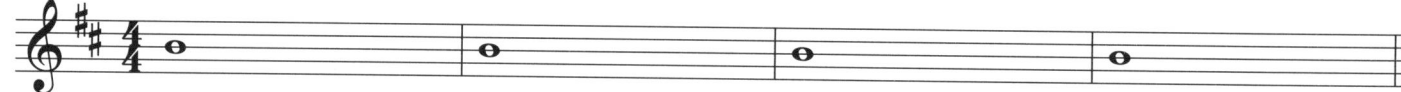

127.

128.
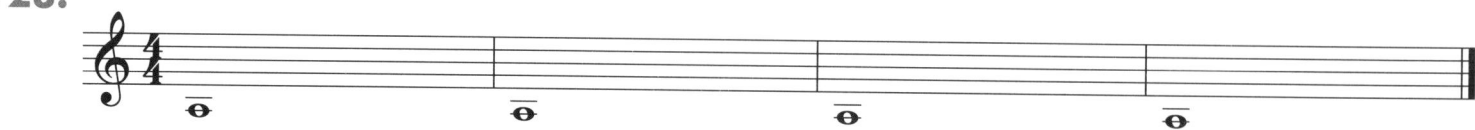

Constant Vibrato Speed

Play each line with a medium steady vibrato.

129. ♩ = 70
1st position
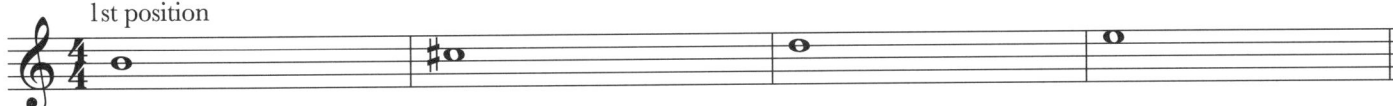

130.

131.
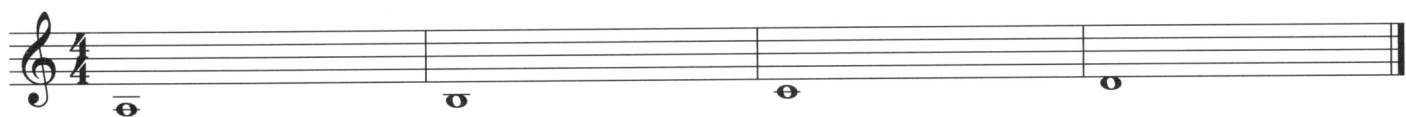

132.
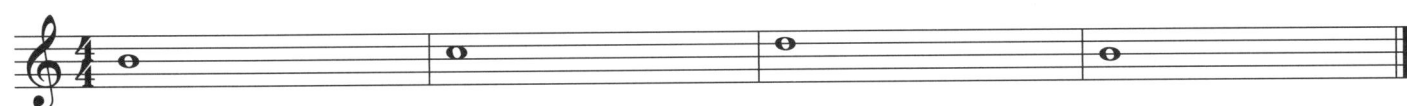

133.
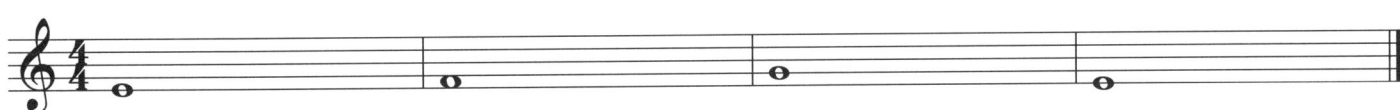

134.
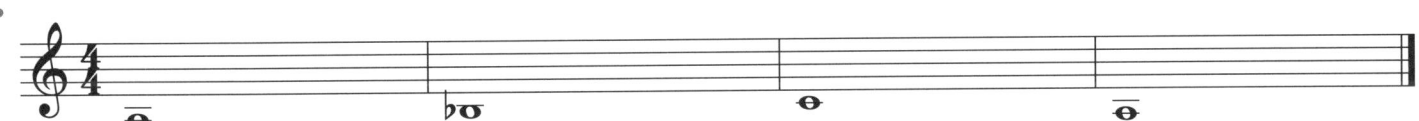

135.
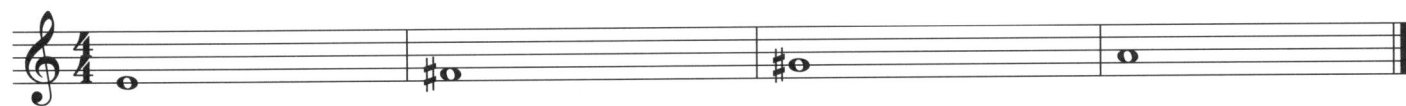

136.
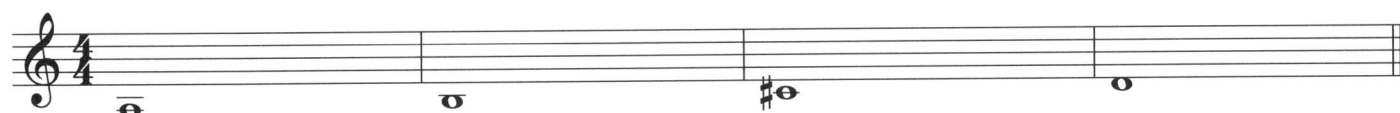

26 Changing Vibrato Speed

137.
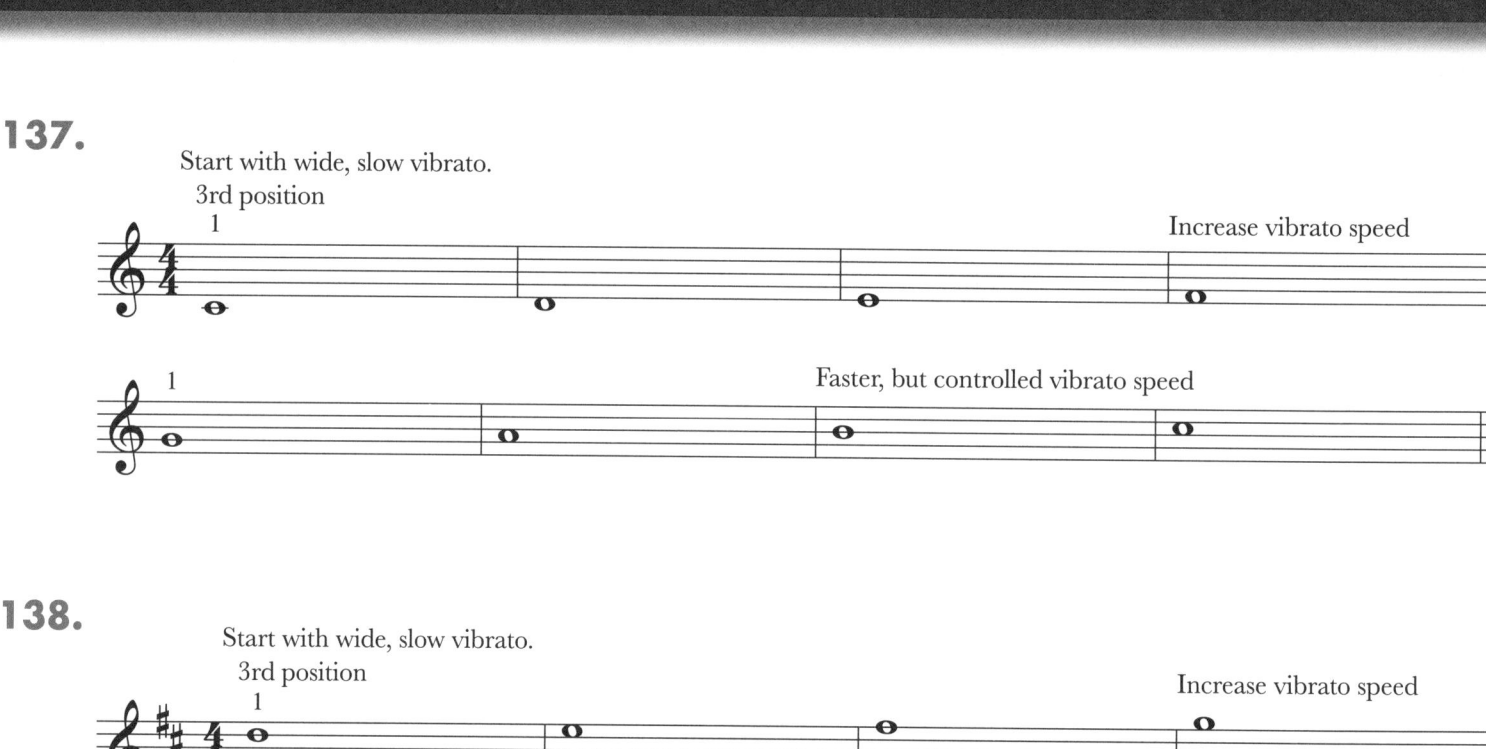

138.

139.

140.
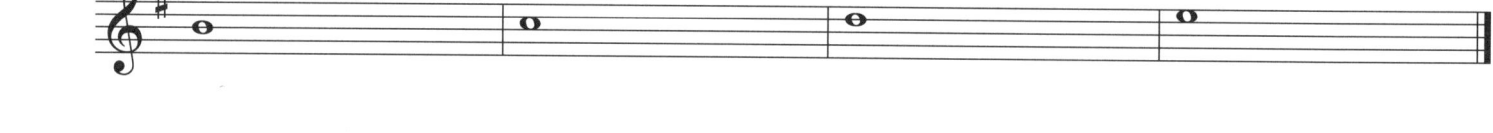

Changing Vibrato Speed

Vibrato will help sustain the sound.

28 Controlling Vibrato Speed

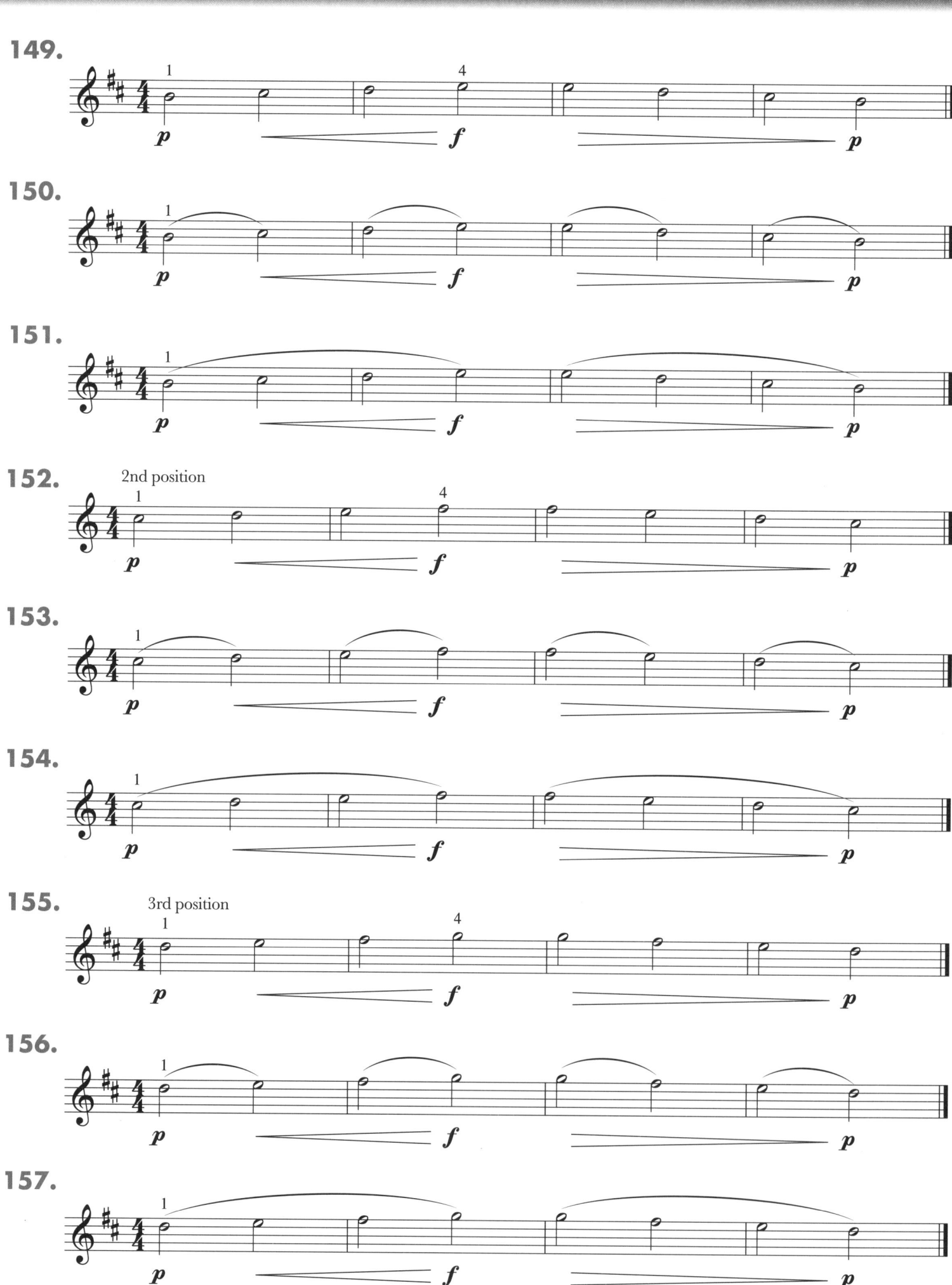

Controlling Vibrato Speed

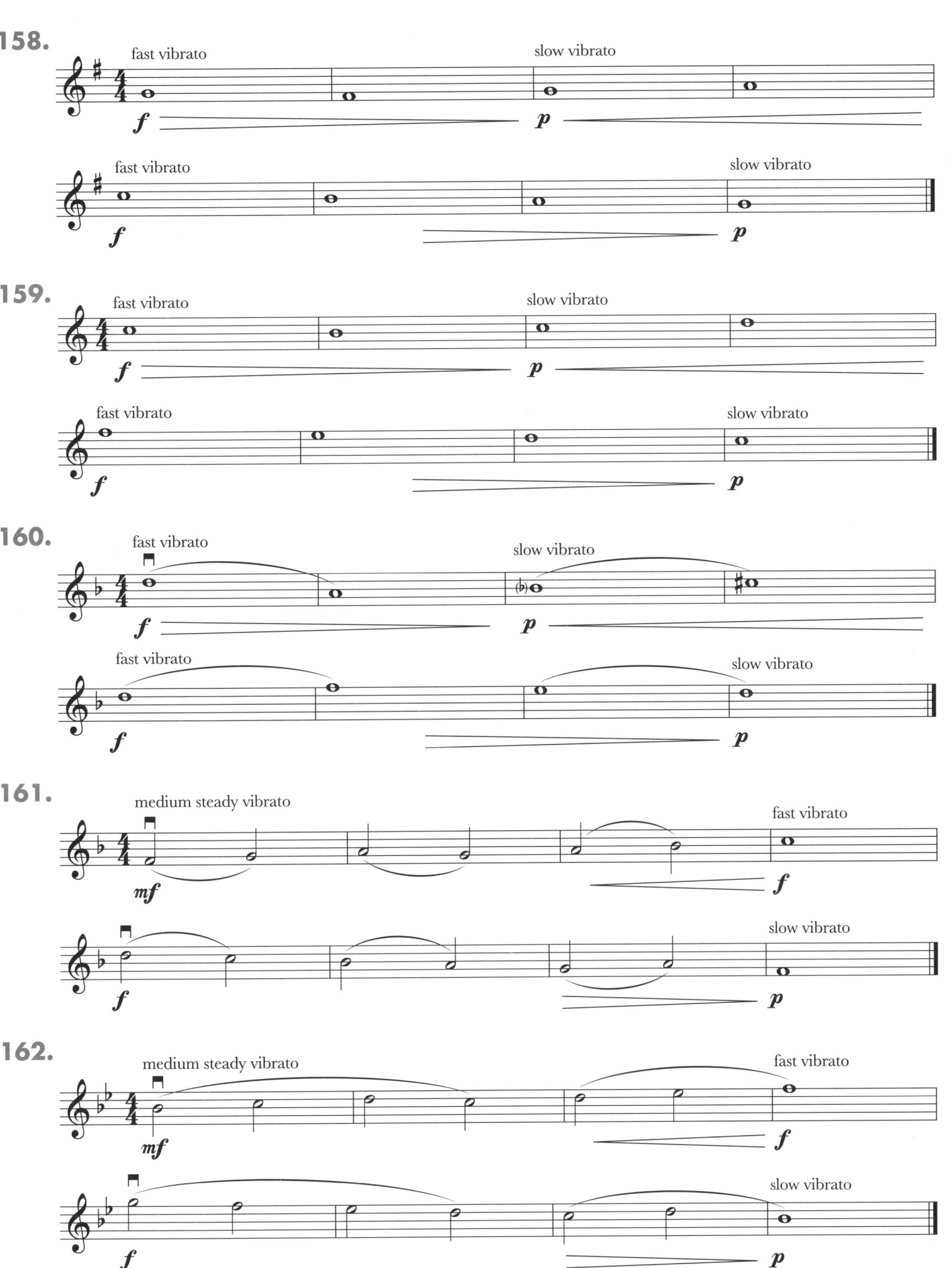

30 Active, Continuous Vibrato

Active, Continuous Vibrato

167. C Major Scale

168. In F Major

169. In B Minor

170. B♭ Major: Thirds & Scale

32 Controlling Vibrato Speed With Dynamics

171. Hills and Valleys

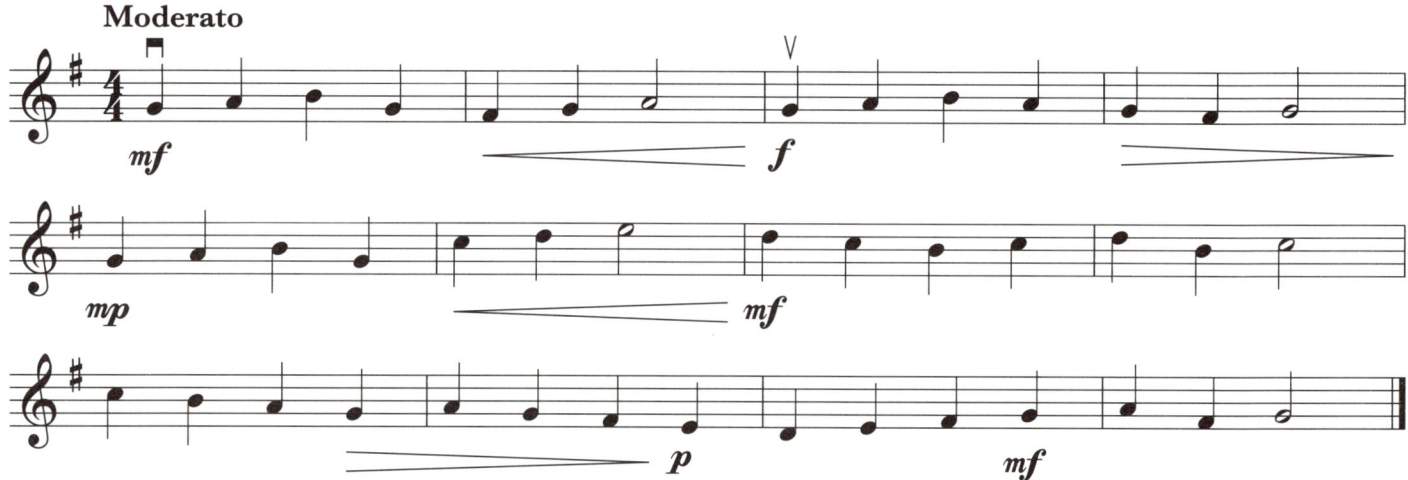

172. The Goblin Waltz

Vibrate while playing softly.

173. The Melancholy Prince

Controlling Vibrato Speed With Dynamics

Video Demo: Ex. 174   33

Vibrate even while playing softly.

174. Quiet Snowfall
Video Demo

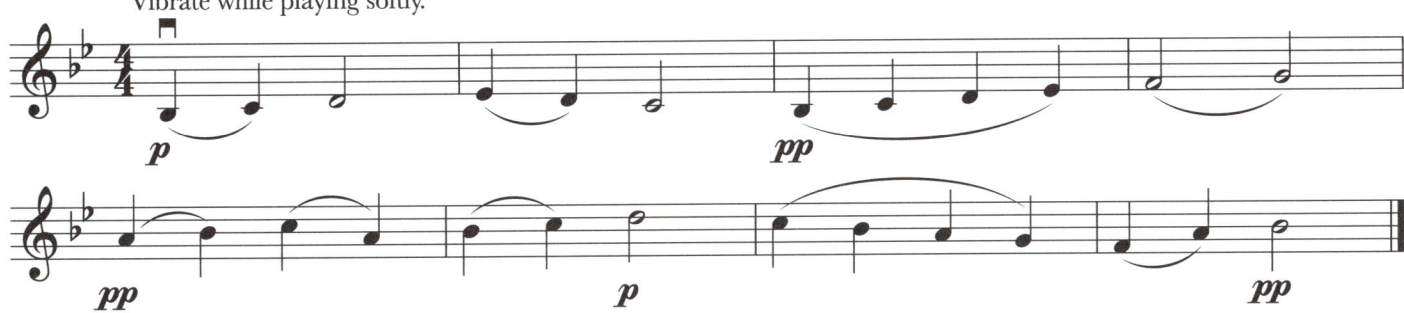

175. Morning Mist

176. Satin Ribbons

177. The Lost City

121VN

34 Active, Continuous Vibrato

178. Bamboo Flute *Chinese Folk Song*

179. Scotland's Burning *Traditional*

180. London Bridge *Traditional*

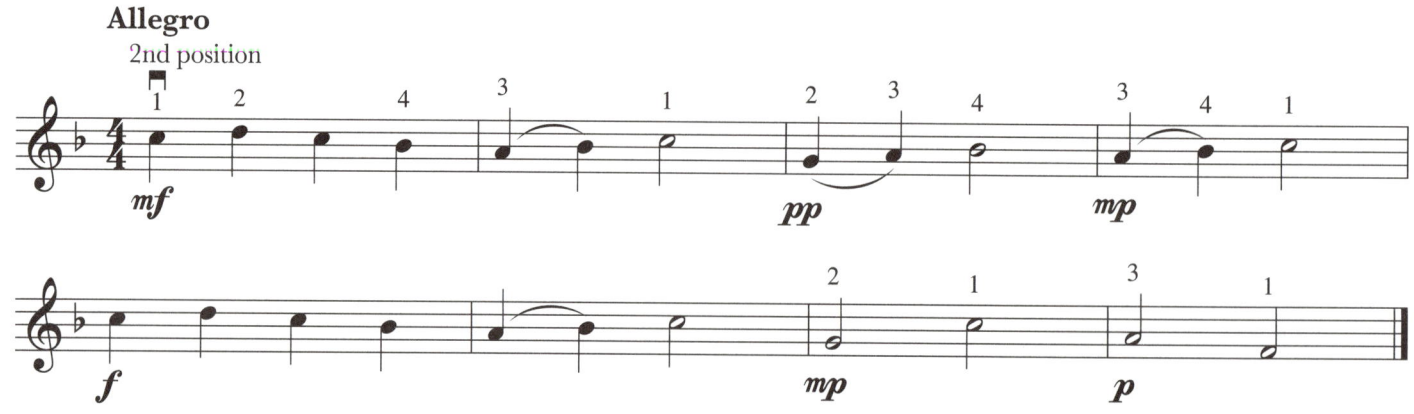

Active, Continuous Vibrato

81. Long, Long Ago *T. H. Bayly*

82. Sicilian Hymn *Traditional*

83. French Folk Song *Traditional*

36 Vibrato on Eighth Notes

Try vibrating on the first eighth note of each set.

Vibrato on Eighth Notes

38 Fast Vibrato Accents

Accent with bow speed and vibrato.

193. Accenting in E Minor

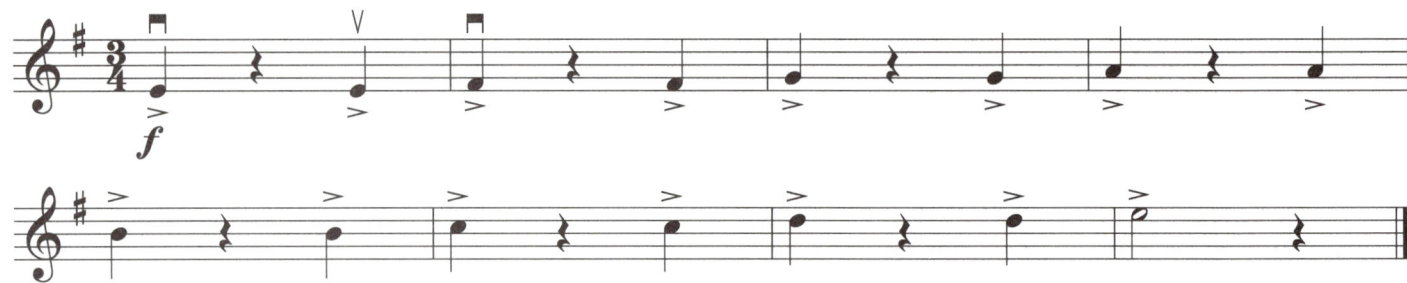

194. Steadfast March

195. Regal Minuet

Fast Vibrato Accents

196. Accenting on Two

197. Yablochko
Russian Folk Song

198. Atlas, Bearer of the Heavens

40 Expressive Vibrato

199. Arioso from Cantata, BWV 156

J. S. Bach

200. Nimrod from Enigma Variations, Var. IX, Op. 36

Edward Elgar

Expressive Vibrato

41

201. Winter from "The Four Seasons," Op. 8, No. 4
Antonio Vivaldi

202. Love Theme from Romeo and Juliet Fantasy Overture
P. I. Tchaikovsky

121VN

42 Expressive Vibrato

203. Londonderry Air
Irish Folk Song

204. Mo Li Hua
Chinese Folk Song

205. Simple Gifts
Shaker Folk Song

Expressive Vibrato 43

206. Gymnopedie No. 1
Erik Satie

207. Ave Maria
Bach/Gounod

121VN

44 Senza Vibrato

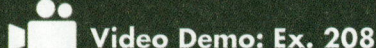
Video Demo: Ex. 208

208. Senza, Slow, Medium, Fast Vibrato

209. A Quiet Place

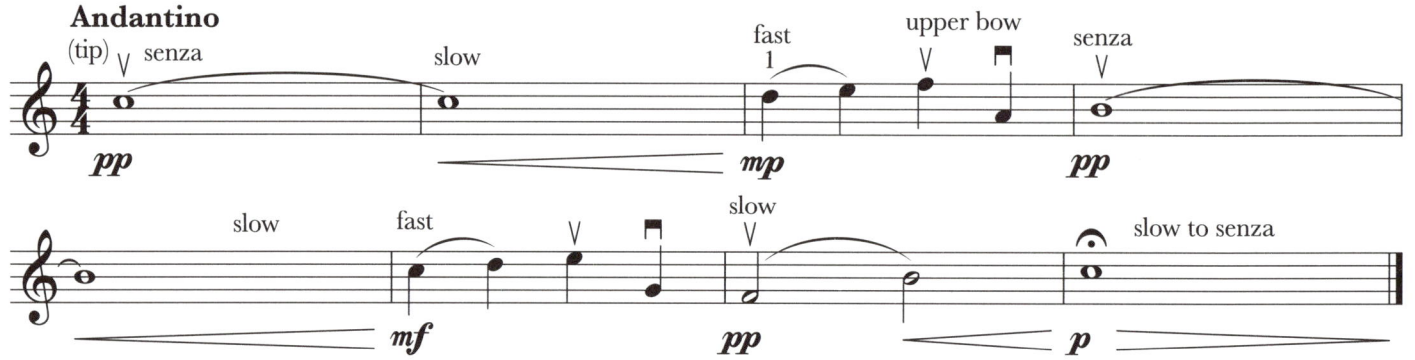

210. Contemplation

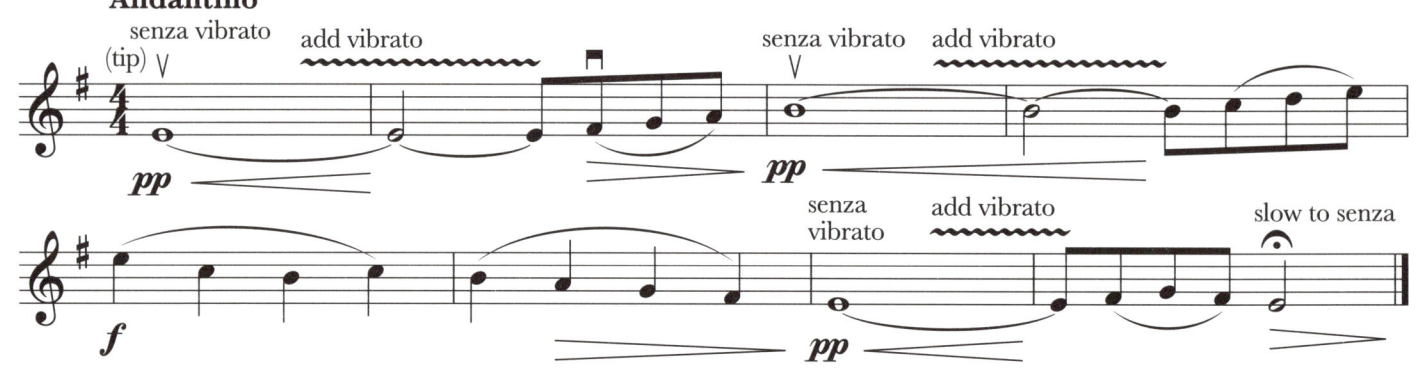

211. Song of Hope

Senza Vibrato

212. Air from "Orchestral Suite No. 3," BWV 1068
J. S. Bach

46 Using Vibrato to Shape Music

213. Meditation from the Opera, "Thaïs"
Jules Massenet

214. Pavane for a Dead Princess
Maurice Ravel

Using Vibrato to Shape Music

47

15. Barcarolle from "The Tales of Hoffmann"
Jacque Offenbach

16. Theme from Symphony No. 5, 2nd Movement (Op. 64)
P.I. Tchaikovsky

121VN

Petite Aria

Jeremy Woolstenhulme